FROM A
STUDIO
IN OAKLAND
CALIFORNIA

ENIA OAKS

From a Studio in Oakland, California: 108 Notes on Existence
Copyright © 2025 by Enia Oaks

All rights reserved. No portion of this book may be reproduced, stored in a retrieval system, or transmitted in any form or by any means—electronic, mechanical, photocopy, recording, scanning, or other—except for brief quotations in critical reviews or articles, without the prior written permission of the publisher.

ISBN 979-8-9987696-0-3 (Hardcover)
ISBN 979-8-9987696-1-0 (Soft cover)
ISBN 979-8-9987696-2-7 (E-book)

Cover and Interior design by Nuno Moreira, NMDESIGN
Printed in the United States of America

FROM A STUDIO IN OAKLAND CALIFORNIA

108 NOTES

ON EXISTENCE

ENIA OAKS

INTRODUCTION

I've spent my life fascinated with the human experience. Even before I could understand or had language for all that I wondered about. Life truly is a wondrous journey that unfolds alongside our consciousness. These writings are the manifestation of my soul's journey through life thus far. By profession, I am an emergency medicine physician, which means I've spent most of my adult life learning how to care for people—not just their bodies, but often their fears, their grief, their quiet hopes. Amidst that, I have observed one common thing we all share: the need to be witnessed. To have someone see us — *really* see us –our fears, our hopes, our struggles, our beauty. That is, I think, one of the deepest longings of the human heart. And perhaps even more tender than being witnessed by others is learning to witness ourselves — with gentleness, with honesty, with reverence.

I wrote this book during a period of my life when it felt like I was witnessing my own soul for the first time in a long while. A period where I had to learn how to sit with my own life — not as a critic or fixer — but as a gentle observer. To honor what was beautiful, and also what was breaking.
And so I offer it to you now —not as expertise — but as a fellow human who has seen the proof that we are never as alone as we feel. I offer it with the hope that you, too, feel seen within these pages.

In some way, we are all hurting and hoping. If this book can offer even a small moment of comfort, clarity, or connection—then it has done what it came here to do. This is an offering in service of humanity—yours, mine, and ours, collectively.

TABLE OF CONTENTS

SELF	15
1. When It's All Said and Done	17
2. The Things That Refuse to Leave Us	18
3. The Universe Knew Me by Name	19
4. Who I Say: Finding Identity	20
5. You Are Not Broken	21
6. Thank You *[for loving me]*	23
7. Arbiter	24
8. Somber	25
9. Vibrance	26
10. Reflection	27
11. We Are Not Here to Endure Life	28
12. The Unspoken Contracts	29
13. The Uncommon	30
14. Letting Go	31
15. Elementary School Portrait	33
16. The Shape of What We Lost	34
17. Escape Artist	35
18. Yosemite	36
19. On Pain	37
20. Wild	38
21. If Not Real	40
22. Soft Soul	41
23. Powerful	42
24. The Sacred Relationship	43

HEALING — 45

- 25. Roadmap Back to Self — 47
- 26. Armor — 49
- 27. Patterns — 51
- 28. Identity Shift — 52
- 29. Dream State — 53
- 30. October — 54
- 31. Emotional Accountability Will Change Your Life — 55
- 32. Certificate of Normalcy — 57
- 33. Somewhere Along the Coast — 58
- 34. Healing Cannot Happen in a Vacuum — 59
- 35. A Love Letter to the Perfectionist — 61
- 36. Self-Love Is the Point — 62
- 37. Kind, Not Weak — 63
- 38. Reckoning — 64
- 39. On Anger — 65
- 40. Pause — 66
- 41. Little at a Time — 67
- 42. Elastic — 68

LOVE AND OTHER PEOPLE — 71

- 43. To Be Seen — 73
- 44. You to Me, Me to You — 75
- 45. On Acceptance — 76
- 46. Deep — 77
- 47. No New Villains — 78
- 48. Relationship Rule #1: *Your Intuition Cannot Be Outsourced* — 80
- 49. Burn — 81

50. Safe Keepers	82
51. Relationship Rule #2: *Learn to See People As Human*	83
52. Because I Love You: *On Grace*	85
53. Pedestals	87
54. Relationship Rule #3: *See the Good in Others, but Let Intuition Guide Alignment*	88
55. Steady State	90
56. Relationship Rule #4: *Nothing That Is Meant for You Will Leave You Empty*	92
57. Grounded	94
58. Coming Home: *On Love*	95
59. Love Feels Like	96
60. Relationship Rule #5: *Just Because You Feel It Strongly Doesn't Make It True*	97
61. Ten Feet Tall	99
62. Relationship Rule #6: *Remain in the Present Moment With Every Connection*	101
63. A Love Letter to the Anxious Heart	103
64. On Rejection	105
65. Relationship Rule #7: *Love Must Be Chosen*	106
66. Me and You	108
67. Love You, *Freely*	109
68. Relationship Rule #8: *Examine Your Resentments, Identify Your Core Needs*	110
69. Love Says	112
70. Relationship Rule #9: *How a Person Feels About Themself Is How They Will Treat You*	113
71. For me: *On Forgiveness*	115

THE JOURNEY OF LIFE   117
  72. And My Soul Said to Me: *"You Said We'd*   119
  Always Be Free"
  73. The Journey of Life   121
  74. What Calls You   122
  75. There Is Only Alignment and Misalignment   123
  76. Calm   124
  77. Salve   125
  78. Good For the Soul   126
  79. Springtime   127
  80. I *Am* Home   128
  81. Metamorphosis   130
  82. When the Sky Splits Open   131
  83. The Fundamental Question   134
  84. Hand Made   135
  85. Why Not Me?   136
  86. Good Fear   137
  87. The Choice   138
  88. Becoming   139
  89. On: Purpose   141
  90. The Sum of a Life Fully Lived   142
  91. You   143

BEAUTY IN EXISTENCE   145
  92. Passing Through   147
  93. Love Letters from the Universe   148
  94. Beauty in Stillness   150
  95. Cinnamon   151
  96. Rituals   153
  97. Balance   154

98. Eclipse	155
99. Release	156
100. Serendipity and Us	157

FARTHER THAN THOUGHT 159

101. Choosing to Believe	161
102. You Do Not Need Permission	163
103. The Truth About Changing Your Life	164
104. Expansion Anxiety	165
105. Where Sky Meets the Ocean	166
106. Meet Me on the Limb	167
107. The One	169
108. What I Would've Told You Sooner	170

SELF

FROM A STUDIO IN OAKLAND CALIFORNIA

WHEN IT'S ALL SAID AND DONE

When it's all said and done, I want to say that I lived.
I want to say that I tried
And risked
And cried.
I want to know that I showed up
And put myself on the line for what I believed in.
I want to know and feel that I gave it my best shot
At being happy
And feeling love
And dancing freely.
When it's all said and done, I want to know
Me.

THE THINGS THAT REFUSE TO LEAVE US

They call these *golden star moments* or core memories. For better or worse, these are the signposts along our life path. They mark the pivots—the moments that shape us.

With each one, we turn either toward love and our truest self, or toward fear and self-protection. Toward deeper connection and appreciation of the richness of life, or toward the quiet loneliness within walls we felt we needed to build. Toward surrender and expansion, or toward resistance and contraction.

Some of these moments arrive in joy: a fleeting instance of perfect alignment, the warmth of a hand in yours, the way the light fell on a childhood afternoon, the smell of asphalt on a summer day as you rode your bike as a moving vestige of freedom. Others arrive in heartbreak; the last time you heard their voice, the phone call that changed everything, the moment of quiet realization that something once so beautiful has fractured beyond repair.

They live in us long after they pass. We carry them, not as burdens, but as proof that we were *here*, that we *felt* deeply, that we existed in the rawest sense of the word. These things that refuse to leave us carry the memories of how *we* came to be.

FROM A STUDIO IN OAKLAND CALIFORNIA

THE UNIVERSE KNEW ME BY NAME

Through all the chaos and pain, your path will still unravel one step at a time. When it feels like the breakdown is inevitable, you will wake, and the days will go on—as if there was no disruption in the ribbon of time. Of the journey. The sun will still smile and touch your arm.

Through the depths and valleys that threaten to end time, the soul underneath will remain. The one that still believes in beauty and harmony. The soul that is resolute in its dignity. Almost as if it knows that something big is looking out after it.

The breeze through the trees will never once utter hate. Only bustling and lively chatter from day to day. The children will still laugh sing-song-like and stare curiously as they do. The rhythmic beautiful dance of life will keep pace and step with the orchestra, gracefully gliding from one corner through; one season to the next.

Your wide-eyed wonder may have known pain from other human beings. But the universe? No, she's only ever known your name. She sings it in tune so melodically. I think it's one of her favorites.

WHO I SAY: FINDING IDENTITY

Want to know how to free yourself? Decide that your identity is whatever you choose it to be, then commit to the part. You see, identity is defined by our repeated patterns and behaviors. That's it. Yes, in order to consistently engage with the deeper levels of self- needed to accomplish this, you will have to confront the inevitable discomfort that will arise. However, these internal battles and conflicts related to choosing how to show up in the world, are your secret. You get to work through these in the safe and quiet within your own being, where no one else can see. And as long as you continue to show up consistently, you will become known as that person. Also during that process you will reinforce within your own psyche that this is your identity. So choose an identity that makes you happy, and feel inspired, and worthy of love. Then go and be it.

FROM A STUDIO IN OAKLAND CALIFORNIA

YOU ARE NOT BROKEN

If you do not know what is wrong with you but are certain that something feels fundamentally wrong, I need you to know that you are not broken. Chances are, the circumstances of your life have separated you from your inner self so deeply that most days you probably could not identify what it is that you authentically feel. Perhaps there is a frightening emptiness, perhaps you are searching for a real feeling to name- any feeling. Or perhaps you can only identify that what you feel is bad. But you should know that there is a way back to wholeness.

It starts with deciding you no longer want to feel the way you do. That is the compass and the driver out. The next exercise will be to re-learn, or learn for the very first time, self-validation. What you need is a witness for your soul. Someone who is watching. Someone who sees you. *Someone who is asking 'How are you?'* Learning self-validation allows you to become your own witness. You do this by practicing identifying and observing your feeling states without judgement in your day-to-day life. Name the shame you feel, name the inferiority, the violation, the injustice. Name the fear, name the sense of weakness or helplessness. Name your excitement, your anticipation, your enjoyment. Name your softness, your love of connection in a moment.

With practice, this validation of self becomes easier and more fluid over time. Feeling states are informed by thoughts and thought patterns. And once you begin to attune yourself to your feelings, you can then trace your steps backward to the thoughts that lead there. Approach these thoughts with genuine curiosity. Earnestly interrogate the stories you carry around-the conclusions you routinely make. Lend yourself grace and understanding as you explore these thoughts and feelings. You have not known better. You were never taught better.

This process tends to have an outward expanding effect: As you become better able to identify, name, and explore your own thoughts and feelings with compassion, you will begin to draw connections between those feeling states and the external forces that contribute to them. This empowers you to become the protector of your soul. You create a refuge inside of your own being. This safety within is what permits your inner self to start to re-emerge authentically. It will feel safe to share its deepest hopes and hurts, its disappointments and desires, its joy and its pain. Your task here is to listen-to remain open. After all, this is you that you are meeting, possibly for the first. Take your time. Explore your depths. This is how you will, slowly over time, find all of the lost pieces of your being.

This is how you will begin to find a connectedness to life and the experience of being alive again.

THANK YOU [FOR LOVING ME]

I was afraid of my demons,
Wondering who would love me with them.
I used to dream that someone would come
and save me.
I fantasized about heroes.
Someone who I could say thank you to for loving me.
Someone who was looking for someone to save.
Ahead I pushed,
looking.
When I finally looked up,
I met the eyes of a fighter,
weary but determined.
I ran my hands across their arms and shoulders.
I looked at their hands,
calloused but capable.
As I stood up, they did as well.
It took but just a moment to realize-
each movement precisely mirrored back.
The hero I had waited for
was the one staring back at me.

ARBITER

The world has been unkind to you. More unkind than any soul should have known. The worst residue left behind are not the scars but rather are in how you have now taken on the task of your own self injustice. You are now the arbiter of pain. You know your way around, like a home where you have your secret tunnels and passageways. Now that you should be free, you roam the underpasses instead. You cry as the sun sets, and then choose again as it rises anew. Yes, pain and punishment are on your authority. But so are freedom and joy. Each time you call out to all that you pray to, they are listening. They hear you and reply, *'don't you see that the monsters have long gone?'*

Where will you go first when you allow yourself to fly?

SOMBER

There is a somber stage of healing that happens when you begin to understand all of the ways different parts of yourself have been misused and mishandled in your life. It feels tragic and poignant—because it is. You will need to acknowledge and cry for these experiences explicitly. Lest they remain embedded in your subconscious, like old splinters. Cry for your lost innocence. And for the ways you did not know any better. Forgive yourself for the times you did know better and chose otherwise. Comfort yourself for the times you could not find your strength because every part of you was doing its best to stay alive. Be proud of yourself that you did not give up. Through it all, however, do not ever allow yourself to fall into the temptation of self-blame. You were never meant to walk through life unscathed. Every wound, every misstep, every moment of injustice was never proof of your failure or unworthiness but rather is evidence of your endurance. You are still here. Still becoming something magnificent. And that in itself is a quiet kind of victory.

VIBRANCE

Seek the things that light your soul on fire. The nights with deep laughs. The relationships that spark your truest self alive. The sounds that make your body move in beautiful, rhythmic resonance. The moments of pure joy. The things that ignite your most earnest curiosity. The things that scare you in the best way—through which you can be the most vulnerable to yourself. Seek the challenges that dare you to fly. The things that your old self would look at and say, *"I didn't know we could do that."* Seek these things because they show you to yourself. For once you truly see yourself, really and truly see, you can't help but to fall madly in love.

REFLECTION

The person you see in the mirror is a picture painted by the world—until you begin to intentionally take control, wiping away what was imposed to reveal what has always been true.

It is the nature of the human experience that we arrive with only a few innate reference points: the intrinsic worth of our existence and the need for sustenance. A baby does not wonder if it is deserving of milk, it simply exists with an understanding that it is supposed to be fed. *This* is the perfect embodiment of our most magnificent existence—an unquestioned sense of worth.

Over time, our image becomes obscured by how the world tells us we *deserve* to be seen. These projections hold no real weight in the truth of who we are, yet they shape the reflection we come to believe in—until we choose otherwise.

Only with intention can we reject these distortions. Only once we take a rag to the reflective surface, and wipe away the stains of conditioning, do we begin to see what was always there: a perfect and whole being, complete and meant to be *loved.*.

WE ARE NOT HERE TO ENDURE LIFE

We are not here to simply endure life. Yes, there is alchemy in pain and struggle, but there is also alchemy in slowness, in softness, in choosing ease where ease is available. In choosing beauty where it is offered. Just because you are capable of navigating hardship does not mean you have to keep choosing it. Through experience, we develop tolerance—we learn to dodge and weave, to survive in environments that test us. The most resilient among us build armor, shielding their inner world from the harsh realities they've had to face. But if we are not careful, we begin to mistake tolerance for contentment, endurance for fulfillment.

The ability to withstand something is not the same as a requirement to keep carrying it. Life is not a test of how much you can endure; it is an invitation to seek what feeds you. Let go of the belief that struggle is proof of your strength, and instead allow yourself to move toward what makes you feel *whole*.

FROM A STUDIO IN OAKLAND CALIFORNIA

UNSPOKEN CONTRACTS

Do not stand out too much.
Find where you are expected to fit and mold yourself into it.
Don't think too hard about what feels uncomfortable.
Choose what feels safe.
Always be proving yourself somehow.
Make sure your truth does not make anyone uncomfortable.
Don't comment on reality; don't ever look it directly in the eyes.
Focus on counting your beans not your exits.
Don't try too hard.
Make sure you don't seem like you're having a hard time.
Care less.
Be modestly provocative.
Not too modest. Not too provocative.
Be interesting enough to invite to dinner,
but keep your topics gracious.
You can be bold as long as it's in the *right* way.
Above all,
make sure you know your place and try not to make any waves.

THE UNCOMMON

People want to feel the uncommon. At the same time the intensity and rawness can be too much for many—perhaps because they do not know if you have reins over your boundaries. Or perhaps it is because they have not liberated themselves enough to truly appreciate the beauty in that which is uncommon. They will be both fascinated and frightened. Lovers may want to touch you but may not know how to hold all that you are. The thing is, in order for life to feel beautiful, you have to believe in beautiful things—that they exist and in all forms. What a much more wonderful existence to believe that love is real, that joy can be authentic, that relationships can have deep trust; that nature is proof of a benevolent universe, and that the quality of experience of the human soul is as important as the physical body it inhabits. And that the most exquisite things in this world are often also, in fact, odd. Those who exist in the uncommon understand these things. And it becomes a self-fulfilling and affirming cycle: the more you seek, the more you experience. The more you experience, the more you feel and then seek. Eventually, ordinary no longer feels compatible with life.

FROM A STUDIO IN OAKLAND CALIFORNIA

LETTING GO

One of the most terrifying feats we can attempt in life is to let go of all we have steadfastly sought to control. We hold on tightly to things because we fear who we might be without them. The truth of life, however, is that energy is constantly moving, and new realities are perpetually being created. This is true whether we hold on tightly to something or let it go. Liberated and harnessed, this energy can fuel a reality of forward motion in our lives. Fearfully bound, it creates one of frustration and futility. We humans can will a great deal through sheer force for some time. Eventually, though, that which is not aligned with the core of our beings—thus was not meant to be ours—will either fall away or consume us in our attempts to hold onto it.

When you hold on tightly to control, you exist in a contracted state. Nothing flows, neither in nor out. Letting go does not mean you remain stagnant. Rather, it allows you to be carried forward by the energy of your core being. It also does not mean surrendering to the worst parts of yourself. It does, however, mean staring at those parts head-on and accepting, without judgment, that they are also a part of you. This is how you make profound breakthroughs because, after all, you cannot reconcile what you do not acknowledge.

Action begets motion, and the laws of physics tell us that the weight of an object has an inverse relationship to its tendency for forward motion. Consequently, the more you hold onto, the heavier you become, and the slower your forward progress. So, practice letting go. As with everything in life, it can be learned with intention. And will, in return, allow you to move into the realities you have always desired.

FROM A STUDIO IN OAKLAND CALIFORNIA

ELEMENTARY SCHOOL PORTRAIT

On the days you feel most lonely, just remember that you are never alone. There is a small child inside of you, living through every single moment with you. Feeling your joy and wonder, feeling your disappointment and pain. Have fidelity to this child. What do they need today? What would expand their mind in the best way? In what ways are they dying to explore this vast and beautiful life? In what ways do they need to know they are safe? How would you show *them* how deeply loved they are? How would you comfort them in the deepest way that *they* never have to fear being alone?

ENIA OAKS

THE SHAPE OF WHAT WE LOST

The beauty of our youth is directly related to the untainted goodness of our humanity. In those early years, we exist in a state of wholeness—soft and untouched by the weight of experience. With each year, the essence of our souls become shaped and molded with new qualities. Our inner being takes on a new form, trimmed down and hollowed at the places where we have lost our baby fat. In their place however, new structure is replaced. Innocence becomes wisdom. Wonder deepens into exploration. Certainty reorients into curiosity. Security expands into resilience. And earnest love is broken apart and, reshaped—first into heartbreak, then into the capacity to hold a love far bigger than we ever imagined.

We do not ever lose any part of ourselves without gaining something in return. We do not break without being remade. What we once were is not erased, but refined, transformed. The shape of what we lose always remains the framework—the architecture—of the people we become.

ESCAPE ARTIST

Running.
The movement became the high
Never stopping to feel
Never stopping to allow
Pain.
Slip through the night and the narrow alleyways
Keep the inner self tucked deep under disguise
Wine and dancing, hazy
Untethered, unmoored
Never still enough to be caught
Never still enough to be touched
Running.
So we can never be
Loved.

ENIA OAKS

YOSEMITE

There's a saying that goes,
"Everywhere you go, there you are."
It was definitely written by someone who learned to disappear.
Because how else do you learn this,
except by being visible only to yourself?

FROM A STUDIO IN OAKLAND CALIFORNIA

ON PAIN

The pain you have felt in service of trying for greater is a good sign. It means that there is something still inside of you that is alive. Something that desires better- that believes in better. Pain challenges you with questions that have been too frightening to ask and loudly declares truths previously too poignant to hear. When you have an experience that breaks you wide open, there is no longer any place to hide from yourself. The light pours in, illuminating the dark corners. You are stripped down to your naked vulnerability and introduced to your bare flesh- to touch and to wash. Greatest of all, pain commands your undivided attention to the parts of you that have long been forsaken and asks, *"Will you love me here?"*

WILD

We often resist things that aim to constrain us because we believe that freedom means the unbridled exercise of our free will. If we have been subject to circumstances that have violated what should have been sacred privacy or agency, one of the effects is that we grow to deeply resent control. We resist anything that we perceive will restrict our sense of freedom- even to the detriment of our own good. Relationships that may otherwise bring healing and life-affirming bonds look like prisons. Routine feels like entrapment. It feels like the wild horse that is our rebellious spirit is the source of our personal power. But the reality is that not learning to tame this aspect of our psyche ends up being a liability in the pursuit of our own happiness. We will create tornadoes that decimate what we attempt to build and call it a natural disaster.

In actuality, *true* freedom is congruency within your being. It is the quiet sense of peace we build in ourselves by living in the way we know we are capable of. We sleep soundly and dream cosmically. Freedom is releasing the weight of injustice that has been thrust upon us and allowing ourselves to once again surrender to what will guide our souls to higher ground. It is allowing ourselves to be lovingly bound to the responsibilities that nurture our character and the undertakings that lead to our personal expansion. Without this internal surrender, we can never honor the routines that would create self-trust. We will always fall short because we will subconsciously refuse to activate our free will toward the goals we set. And without self-trust, we will only ever feel comfortable living lives that do not challenge us.

Trusting in yourself means that you believe in what you say and what you intend. You are able to soothe the revolts of a wounded soul and gently reassure it that you only intend to lead it toward an expanded and enriched existence. Consequently, you forge an ability to show up in a directed, aligned, and consistent way; because you understand that accountability and integrity to self are paramount to creating your most beautiful life.

ENIA OAKS

IF NOT REAL

What am I meant to be, if not whole?
Why can life mean, if not real?
Where do I go, if not home?
Who do I become, if not me?

FROM A STUDIO IN OAKLAND CALIFORNIA

SOFT SOUL

The truth is that you get to keep your soft soul despite the hardness in this world. You also cannot make anything into what it is not. That is the real task in this life-the seeing. When we keep finding ourselves in old painful patterns, there is something within us that we are not seeing. Very commonly, there is something that we are not willing to look at. But no truth will kill you. It can only set you free if you allow it. So allow yourself to see. Seek truth. It is the seeing that over time becomes sharpened into discernment, which then grows into wisdom. This wisdom will guide your soul to the places where it is safe to be tender- the gardens where it will be watered and flourish. Your life is yours alone to live. To experience. And it is much more beautifully *exquisite* when lived with an open heart.

POWERFUL

Honor your sensuality as this is the pulse of your life force. Treat its expression as sacred, for within it lies the rawest, most potent essence of your being. It is both your creator and your primal feeler, the alchemist that transforms energy into life, longing into creation, and presence into divinity. To deny it is to deny the fire that animates you. To embrace and protect it is to step fully into the power of your own existence. So honor it and it will magnify you in return.

FROM A STUDIO IN OAKLAND CALIFORNIA

THE SACRED RELATIONSHIP

Your relationship with self must be held as sacred in order to heal and fully actualize into the person you are meant to be. This means that you treat your words, thoughts, and behaviors toward yourself as deeply consequential and meaningful—because they are. You stand up for yourself, and you have your own back. You nurture your psyche and treat your dreams and aspirations as implicitly legitimate—because they are. You develop good and healthy habits because your body and soul deserve good things. You cheer on the child inside of you who is bravely navigating this world because they need it. You do not compromise your standards or boundaries for your emotional wellbeing with anyone because it is not up for negotiation. Just as your skin serves as a life supporting barrier for your body, your psyche serves as the life affirming barrier for your soul. Build it through consistent and intentional thoughts and actions, and your soul can only flourish.

HEALING

FROM A STUDIO IN OAKLAND CALIFORNIA

ROADMAP BACK TO SELF

A commonly misunderstood thing about healing is that you actually feel worse before you begin to feel better. Oftentimes, a lot worse. Particularly if your wounds have been buried so deep within yourself that you did not even know some of them existed.

You chip away slowly at the cemented walls that have enclosed them. When you encounter a new insight—an understanding that shifts something within you—there will be an overwhelming wave comprising of awe, relief, vindication, anger, and sorrow. These sensations will wash over you like a long overdue bath. The sorrow is the result of a somber realization of the torment your soul has been experiencing in the shadows. You'll weep because it's tragic and unjust.

Amid this sorrow, you may begin to question if you are even healing at all. After all, you've never felt *this* bad before. But just know that you are. You may begin to question beliefs you have had about yourself and the universe. And the pictures you once saw clearly will begin to fade into amorphous blurs of color. This is good. This dissolution creates space and your questioning is the compass to higher ground.

The truth is that the lives we lead are created by our own perspectives, perceptions, and beliefs. Truly. So, anything that makes you question your beliefs is actually offering you a portal to a greater truth—a more whole existence.

On the other side of each emotional reconciliation process will be a new awareness of self and the world. With this new awareness you can start deconstructing a reality that no longer serves you, and building a new one, piece by piece. It will be important that you maintain an awareness and reverence for this journey because the world will not stop for your healing. You will be challenged and tempted to regress because some of the pillars of your present life are directly dependent on you remaining exactly the same; even if it is killing you from the inside out. The most predatory of beneficiaries may attempt to obfuscate truth because it would allow for your liberation. Keep your eyes steady.

Because the greatest truth of all is that you have always been intrinsically worthy of love and happiness. Your task in this life is to become deeply convicted of this. This truth is your lighthouse though the dark. Write it indelibly. Meditate on it. Because every other good thing you desire flows from this belief.

This is how you heal. This is how you find your way back home.

ARMOR

Some wounds you have will feel like armor. Work on undoing them anyway. If you had to survive in environments that preyed on your vulnerability, you have likely become extremely skilled at being invulnerable. The beauty of this is that you have effectively alchemized what was meant to break you into a sort of superpower. The problem is that, in many cases, this armor becomes impenetrable to even yourself. You find that even you are locked out of the deepest recesses of your inner being, where your most honest desires are held. You learn to perform around them, just tap dancing *right outside* of the truest form of yourself.

Often these traits develop in childhood, where there is no agency in controlling the outside world. However, as adults, these traits are only useful in that you have the capacity to activate them if needed. But in most cases, they only functionally serve to limit your life. You will find that you keep crashing head on into them whenever you try to reach for something that requires your softness and access to the most vulnerable parts of your soul. The goal in healing is not to become defenseless, but rather to develop the ability to discern what *true* danger looks like, and how to feel strength in your softness. In reality, many of these traits never truly leave you, but you are the one who gets to choose the way you show up in the world.

Choose the path that allows for a life of inner liberation, to dream as large as you can imagine. And the one that the child beneath the armor would want to have. They deserve that. Choose the path that allows you to feel connected to yourself and the people who love you. Choose your joy, and your sincerity. And the experiences that allow you to feel connected to your humanity. Choose the path that allows for your wholeness.

FROM A STUDIO IN OAKLAND CALIFORNIA

PATTERNS

You can't always draw a line from patterns to specific outcomes, but you can always draw a line from patterns to present reality. What this offers you is an opportunity to look at the individual parts of your present life that are not what you would want for yourself and explore them from a lens of curiosity. Just like a detective gathering clues, you can often trace your way back to the points of disconnect. From here, you can begin the process of softening— learning that true safety does not come from impenetrability, but from knowing you can trust yourself to navigate life as both strong and open. The past may have shaped you, but you are not bound to it. The patterns may have protected you, but you are free to rewrite them at any point and when they no longer serve you. After all, healing is not about condemning or discarding who you had to become to survive—rather, it is about learning to comfort and integrate all parts of yourself in a way that serves the life you want, and deserve, to live now.

IDENTITY SHIFT

If you find yourself caught between the person you have been and the person you desire to become, you will need to keep your eyes forward and your intentions clear. Our identities are typically the ones we have learned in life will gain us the most love or acceptance. Once we start to heal, however, and truly start loving ourselves, something beautiful occurs: our inner selves begin to merge with our outer identities. In this process we start shedding the identities that do not feel aligned with the core of our being. The difficulty comes in the fact that we as humans are wired for love and connection. When our environment has become accustomed to a certain version of us, it triggers deep existential anxiety to attempt to change. So, often times, we find that our identities will glitch back and forth between old and new. When this occurs, do not condemn yourself and do not become discouraged. This is normal and expected. You are after all seeking exactly what you are wired for: to be loved. However, once you recognize that you have fallen back into an identity performance you no longer align with, it is up to you to pivot back toward your desired state of being.

FROM A STUDIO IN OAKLAND CALIFORNIA

DREAM STATE

What does it mean to want everything and nothing all at once?
                    To feel everything
                                      and nothing.

    What does it mean to eat and never feel a full belly?

How about to breathe
            but still gasp like you are running at full sprint?

      What does it mean to sleep but never find rest?
Or to speak and never say a word?

What does it mean to touch your own flesh but never know if it's real
                                      or a figment
                        of some dream
      You don't know how to wake from.

OCTOBER

The sun and the wind slow danced until dusk

I stayed until I could no longer find meaning
In the shadows

FROM A STUDIO IN OAKLAND CALIFORNIA

EMOTIONAL ACCOUNTABILITY WILL CHANGE YOUR LIFE

If you want to change your life, take radical accountability for your life circumstances. Take complete ownership over your emotional being and its role in shaping your reality. It feels deeply unfair the ways we have been hurt by the unkindness in this world. And the way that life does not wait for us to be ready first before it gives us challenges that shake us to our core. It does not seem right that we inherit the trauma of our ancestors through cycles of harm perpetuated by those who were supposed to care for us. Or that we can be born into circumstances and bodies that stack the deck so high against us before we've even begun to play.

The truth is that these aspects of life *are* deeply unfair. In a perfect world, we would all be given the same circumstances, environments, tools, and gifts. We would be nurtured and supported toward our highest potential. And we'd never have to know the feeling of being told we are not good enough. However, the very nature of being alive requires that we encounter forces that mold our existence. This is true for all living entities on earth. And while our indignation may be valid, it does not change this reality.

It is natural to feel anger, inadequacy, pity, or even defeat when we find ourselves in low places we did not earn. But the way we adapt and evolve in response to these feelings determines the reality of our lives. Unless we take accountability for how we navigate our pain, we will remain perpetual victims of our circumstances.

This is emotional accountability: taking ownership of your role in your life circumstances rather than externalizing and projecting the causes as something outside of yourself. The places where we have made choices that have directly led to our present. The moments we chose to give into our impulses or ego over our wisdom. The ways that we allow self-pity to enable our self-harm. The times we surrendered our power to narratives that only kept us bound.

This is one of the most difficult aspects of healing, because it requires accepting responsibility for your own shortcomings, vices, and wounded underbelly. Having these aspects of your person do not make you bad. They make you human. You are still worthy of love and beauty, grace, and healing.

When you externalize the causes of your circumstances, you also disempower yourself from changing them. But the moment you recognize your own agency—the moment you realize that you *can* shape your reality—is one of the most powerful awakenings of your life. Suddenly, solutions appear where before were only problems. You begin to see freedom where once was only bondage. Most importantly, you commandeer the pen the write your own life story.

FROM A STUDIO IN OAKLAND CALIFORNIA

CERTIFICATE OF NORMALCY

On this day and every day forward, you are officially recognized as *human*.

All that you have feared was too unlovable, too painful, too strange—it turns out fits right into the fabric of humanity. It has been felt before. Lived before. Survived before. The deepest, most secret burdens you carry are proof that you belong here. To a human race that struggles with longing, unworthiness, self-doubt, and fears of inadequacy. You are in the right place.

Shame lied to you when it said that you were the only one. The truth is, we are all bound together by common threads that make us more alike than not. You are not *the only one*, and you never were. So set down the burden of believing that whatever it is you feel ashamed about makes you an outsider. It does not and you are not. You are simply and beautifully, *human*.

ENIA OAKS

SOMEWHERE ALONG THE COAST

Let's take a drive through the mountains,
                      by the coast,
    and look at all of the places
where I found the meaning
of heartbreak
      and grace.
           And understood that the reflections in the water
                  turn into ripples with the pebbles.

          Let's go for some time
     so I can understand again
what it means to see God
    in the colors in the sky
        and feel like I could take flight.

              Let's go back
    to where we met ourselves in the trees.
    And feel once again
        what it meant
           to be free.

FROM A STUDIO IN OAKLAND CALIFORNIA

HEALING CANNOT HAPPEN IN A VACUUM
On Trust

On your journey to find wholeness, I hope you will allow yourself to learn trust and openness once again. I hope that you will choose to navigate the waters of your life, to ride the seas—rather than hiding away at dock. I hope you will dare to break through the upper limits of your joy that were nailed in place by your traumas.

You see, a fundamental truth of life is that we are meant to love and be loved. Our survival and happiness require it. And there is no love without trust. There is a version of contentment where you observe life from a distance, peering through the drapes, allowing in only the amount of connection needed to quiet the ghosts in your mind. In this version, you exchange trust for vigilance, and you never truly find rest. In contrast, while contentment does not require trust, happiness cannot exist without it. To be truly happy, you must be willing to surrender to the unknown of life. This is how it can surprise you with all of the goodness that it has to offer. Because, happiness cannot be controlled for; it can only be allowed in time and time again.

So I hope you choose to learn how to trust again. I hope you choose it because it is the highest vote of confidence in yourself and the clearest sign that you are ready for your most beautiful life. At its core, choosing to trust another is actually choosing to trust yourself—that come what may, you will love yourself through it.

That you will be okay.

You never deserved those experiences that robbed you of your ability to trust. But you do deserve wholeness and to release all of the heaviness you have carried for so long. I hope you choose that.

FROM A STUDIO IN OAKLAND CALIFORNIA

A LOVE LETTER TO THE PERFECTIONIST

You learned to perfectly perform in order to earn love, only to find that this exact quality is what others now resent about you. How can that be? Your perfection was never rooted in vanity; it was survival. A carefully honed skill to secure safety and belonging. Yet the more effortlessly you seem to execute, the more others assume you never had to bleed for it. They don't see the weight you carry, only the finished product, and for that, they turn away.

And so, now you wear their disdain like a fresh wound, something new to atone for, as if your perfectionism betrayed you. You perform to feel good enough, then downplay your performances to feel accepted. But proving your humanness is not your cross to bear. Your only responsibility is to care for the soul beneath the striving, to soften where you've hardened, and to continue to remind yourself that love was never meant to be earned. We are all inherently worthy of it, so it was only ever meant to be received.

SELF-LOVE IS THE POINT

When we start on this journey to heal ourselves, we inevitably reach a place where we feel functional enough to navigate our lives and relationships. It is at this place that we may begin to wonder, *What is the meaning of our continued pursuit for healing? Where does it all lead?* But then we remember the way that we do not get triggered in the same ways we once did. We see how our shoulders hang more easily and our laugh comes more naturally. We notice how we feel safe within our own bodies. And how the judgments of other people no longer affect our sense of self-worth. We observe how our voice is louder and more self-assured. And how we can now instinctively access and honor our deepest level of knowing. When we notice all these things, we begin to understand that there is no final destination to our healing, rather it is in continued service of our state of existence. It is then that it becomes clear that self-love—a true and deep love for ourselves—is and has always been the point.

KIND, NOT WEAK

Don't you ever mistake kindness for weakness. Being kind does not mean bowing your head, making yourself small, or letting others trample on you just to keep the peace. Kindness does not mean giving to the point of depletion. Or remaining in harmful spaces simply because it is what is expected of you. Kindness is not blind forgiveness. Or self-abandonment in the name of being "good." Real kindness is strength wrapped in softness. It means carrying yourself with dignity even when the world tries to harden you. It means personal emotional accountability. Kindness requires firm boundaries and a willingness to say no. It is refusing to tolerate disrespect but choosing integrity where your ego wants revenge. It is not prostrating yourself, but it is reading a room. Above all, kindness is holding yourself accountable and treating those around you by the standard of what is good for the soul, yours and theirs.

ENIA OAKS

RECKONING

No more.
No more emotional self-betrayal.
No more willful subversion of your intuition.
No more accepting what does not feel honorable.
No more saying yes when you mean no, saying no when you mean yes.
No more waiting for someone else to choose you before you choose your best life.
No more justifying mistreatment because you understand where it comes from.
No more settling for closeness when what you need is connection.
No more standing between someone and their consequences.
No more hunching yourself over to make yourself smaller.
No more mistaking your empathy for obligation.
No more pretending that you didn't notice that.
No more over-explaining your boundaries.
No more of what is not humane.
Simply no more.

FROM A STUDIO IN OAKLAND CALIFORNIA

ON ANGER

Be mindful of your anger, taking care to notice what it is that causes you to feel deeply incensed. Oftentimes, this is pain being invulnerably expressed. It is far easier to shout than to admit that your feelings have been hurt. So it often is revealing where your vulnerabilities have been trampled on. For some it is easier to suppress the emotion entirely because they were never taught healthy expression, so they fear its intensity. However, a healthy and whole existence is not one without anger. Rather it is one that seeks wisdom in all emotions but does not allow itself to become lost or consumed in the emotion. It seeks healthy rather than destructive exploration and release. Used effectively, anger will show you the parts of yourself that feel dishonored, your soul's deepest sensitivities and wounds. It will give you the fire to liberate yourself from that which threatens the wellbeing of your soul. Anger can be your soul's most loyal ally, if you are careful to extract its wisdom and contain its wrath.

PAUSE: ON DISCERNMENT

Learn to pause. Practice it. Let it become second nature. Pausing is not passivity—it is a profound act of trust in yourself and an exercise of deep wisdom. When faced with a decision, an opportunity, or even a conflict, resist the urge to react immediately. Not every feeling is a call to action. Most are not. Pausing allows you to step outside the urgency of the moment and recognize what is real.

Practice naming your feelings in the moment. Learn to say: *I feel frustrated. I feel disappointment. I feel unappreciated. I feel irritable. I feel* rejected. To name your feelings as they occur is to short-circuit the emotional pathways related to those feelings. It individuates your observational state from your feeling state. You become both the experiencer and the observer, the one feeling and the one witnessing. This small but powerful shift creates *just* enough separation to give you the potency that comes with the observer state: the power to choose *how to experience and respond* to the emotion rather than just *reacting* to them.

It is in the space, in the absence of movement, that truth is often clarified and fortified. What is true and right for you will still be so on the other side. What is false or incomplete will either reveal itself or breakdown in the pause. So learn to use this. To pause and observe. Your life will be richer and more aligned for it.

LITTLE AT A TIME

On the days you can only manage to put one foot in front of the other, just do that and know that it is okay. The universe is not crashing down. You are not failing. This is not the breakdown you feared was inevitable. This is your human form. Tired but very much alive. Nurture and pour as much love as you can muster inward and know *that* is enough. The sun always rises, every tide turns, and your strength will return. Your light will return. But for this moment just know that you are—*just as you are*—enough.

Affirmation:

On the days when all I can do is put one foot in front of the other, — I will do that and let it be enough. I trust that nothing is falling apart beyond repair. The universe is not crashing down. I am not failing. I am not breaking in the way I once feared. I am human. Tired, but deeply and undeniably alive. I choose to pour love inward. I choose to be gentle with myself. To tend to myself here. I trust that my strength will return. That my light will return. And that this tide will turn. Until it does, — I will let myself exist exactly as I am and know that I am enough.

ENIA OAKS

ELASTIC

How you know you are healing:

Hurt will still come
but it no longer devours you whole.
You won't have to name it as strength,
you will just notice how you stay,
with yourself
until the ache lets go.

You will name what you are feeling
without reaching for a reason.

You will pat yourself down
to know you are safe;
to give your psyche proof.

You won't need to explain it away,
or bury it under stories.
You will just know that it was never personal.

You will touch your own arm
like someone you love
and speak to the child inside you
who once didn't know what to do with the pain.

FROM A STUDIO IN OAKLAND CALIFORNIA

The fire storms will come and pass,
not because the flames were not real,
but because you chose not to disappear into them.
You chose instead to summon the rain.

This is what you've learned.
How   to   *bend*
and how to return.

You did not become immune.
You just became
elastic.

LOVE AND OTHER PEOPLE

TO BE SEEN

In friendship and in love, we are granted the first sacred experiences of being witnessed. Of being seen for our essence. It is often in another's gaze that we first catch a glimpse of ourselves. We are able to see our wounds, and our shimmer, our idiosyncrasies, and our shadows. It is here we first feel real because someone else has seen us as such. This is why the first love or friendship heartbreak often undoes us. It is the mirror saying, "Yes, you exist. And yes, you are worthy to be loved." But it is also the mirror that can break us. Because when that reflection shatters, we wonder if we will do too. But this is far from where the story ends.

The most powerful becoming in life is learning to be your own witness. Learning to see yourself—clearly, wholly, gently—without needing a reflection from anyone else. *This* is the sacred space of self-possession.

It is the moment you stop asking love to save you. And instead, *you* become the love that stays. You stop needing your being to be reflected to understand *who* you are. And to become the one who sees yourself fully, is to become free.

Because the love you find from this place is different. It does not arrive to build you. Or rescue you. Or make you feel real. It arrives because you already are. And *you* recognize it because you already are.

It sees you. Not because it gives you permission to see yourself, but because *you* showed up in full form.

Already home.

YOU TO ME, ME TO YOU

One beautiful thing about love is that when someone shows you love, it is because they have learned it from someone else who loved them in that way. The way their mother soothed them when they were falling apart. The way their father always reassured them that all is not lost. The way their sister cracked just the right joke to make them smile when they were feeling low. And the way their best friend just climbed down and sat with them in their sadness. The act of truly loving someone is to give them a piece from the most beautiful part of your soul, which is an amalgamation of the beautiful parts of many souls. In the best way, it is the sincerest wish for happiness, protection, and wholeness to be ever-present in their life. They get to take and keep that as part of themselves forever. In this way, love is passed from, heart to heart, community to community, generation to generation. And that when we are loved by someone, we are also being loved by all of the beautiful intentions that have ever encircled them.

ON ACCEPTANCE

We are social creatures, who crave community and acceptance. Our wellbeing and humanity require it. However, the truth is that people can only accept you in so much as they have accepted themselves. Someone who hates themselves cannot love you. And those who project hatred to others do not love themselves.

The kindest and most openhearted people are not that way because they are innately morally superior. Rather, they are that way because they have learned how to accept themselves fully, which implicitly means that they have also learned how to control their most harmful impulses. It is from this place of self-acceptance that they can now extend love and inclusion outwardly. Once you understand this about other people, it becomes easier to understand that their actions towards you often have very little to do with you and everything to do with the conditions inside of their own soul.

There is a place of abundant acceptance for every single soul on this planet, so if you find yourself in a place that feels more rejecting than inviting, this is your sign to keep pouring love inward and to keep moving forward. The right spaces and people will meet you where you are most free.

DEEP

The bad news? People can only meet you as deeply as they've met themselves. The good news? People can meet you as deeply as they've met themselves. If depth is what you are after, seek out those who are already diving into their own pools, journeying deeper and deeper into their wells of understanding about themselves. People who have learned to swim in their own waters. The ones unafraid of shadows and contradiction. *These* are the people who can meet you underwater.

NO NEW VILLAINS

Once you decide that you are no longer interested in creating any additional villains in your life story, it becomes easier to release people where they are and without malice.

The truth is that everyone is on their own life path, and we are all on our own grand journeys. We all have our sharpened edges that we needed to get through the darkest nights. Some were dealt the most unfair of circumstances. Others endured unspeakable trauma and horrors. But the process of healing is essentially learning how to file down those edges. It is painful and requires the courage to hold yourself accountable for the ways you have been the villain to yourself and others. But you do it so you can have the beautiful things you have always wanted, without fear of destroying them or destroying yourself.

In that process too, however, you learn to recognize the sharpened edges of others. You give them grace because you imagine what they have endured. But you release them from a place of humility and understanding. Not because you are not capable of putting up a good fight, but because you are on a different path now. *A path that no longer requires war.* Your humility reminds you that your strength is not impenetrable, that your commitment to healing is not invincible. It must be nurtured and protected.

But the understanding also tells you that the patterns that create would-be-villains need a stage to play out.

What a powerful thing to realize that your life story is yours to write.

RELATIONSHIP RULE #1
Your Intuition Cannot Be Outsourced

Do not hand over the reins of your safety or emotional well-being to anyone else. This is not to say that you should not trust people as trust creates some of the most beautiful experiences in this life. But you should never substitute someone else's judgment for what feels safe and right for your soul. People, by nature, are inherently self-serving, even when they mean well. Their perspective will always be shaped by their own needs, desires, and biases. This does not make them bad; it simply makes them human. However, it does mean that no one can be a more reliable guardian of your innermost well-being than you. Your intuition exists for a reason. It is a compass, dialed in by your lived experiences, your deepest knowing, and your most primal instincts. It is not a group project, and it does not require validation. It is yours alone, so listen to it. Trust it. Honor it. Let it be the loudest voice in your mind. Because at the end of the day, it is you who must live within the reality of your life. No one else can bear that responsibility with you. So allow your intuition to guide you to the most beautiful version of it.

FROM A STUDIO IN OAKLAND CALIFORNIA

BURN

Some bridges will need to be intentionally lit on fire in order for you to heal and grow into the person you are meant to be. You will know these by the way they consume without any intent to give, and by the way they demand you remain dysfunctional to maintain the relationship. Walking away may initially feel like a loss, but in reality, it is liberation. It is the reclaiming of your energy, your peace, and most powerfully, your right to evolve. Most connections are not meant to be kept for a lifetime; rather many are meant to be lessons that teach you how to choose yourself.

SAFE KEEPERS

Learn to share the most precious parts of your soul only with those who have earned it through lived trust and time. Those who have shown the capacity to hold these parts with care. You will know these people by the safety they create around themselves for everyone they encounter. And by the way they will never pry about your deepest pain. These will be the people whose generosity of spirit you can feel through their words and presence. And the space they will allow for you to open up as much as feels safe for you. The ones who treat trust as sacred. Being vulnerable with them won't feel like a risk or a thrill—it won't feel like something you're chasing or proving. It will not feel illicit. Instead, it'll just feel right, like an easy invitation to be yourself. These are the kinds of people to share with because they will safe guard your heart in the same way they have learned to safe guard their own.

FROM A STUDIO IN OAKLAND CALIFORNIA

RELATIONSHIP RULE #2:
Learn to See People As Human

We cling tightly to the idea of people as either heroes or villains when we do not trust our ability to care for ourselves. We search for someone to save us when we do not believe we are capable of saving ourselves. And look for someone to blame when we haven't learned that emotional accountability does not mean accepting responsibility for the bad things that happen to us. From this perspective, we begin to see the world in absolutes—dividing people into categories of good or bad, saints or villains, saviors or threats. But no human being falls squarely into one category. The very nature of being human is to carry both light and shadow, kindness and imperfection, wisdom and wounds. This is true of every single person on earth. When we label someone as wholly good or wholly bad, we not only deny them their complexity—we deny ourselves the responsibility of recognizing our own role in this mutual dynamic.

To truly see someone, we must be willing to see them in their entirety—not as an ideal to worship, or as a villain to blame, but as a person, flawed and evolving, just as we are. When we learn to see people as human, we free ourselves from the illusion and weight of projected expectations of perfection and the burden of disillusionment. We are able to have more grace, allowing others to be who they are rather than who we expect them to be. In doing this, we learn to see the world in a much more balanced way. The next task then becomes to *assume responsibility for what we allow in our lives*. By reframing our perspective in this way, we make room for real connection—the kind built not on projection, but on alignment and understanding. And we also empower ourselves in affecting our reality.

FROM A STUDIO IN OAKLAND CALIFORNIA

BECAUSE I LOVE YOU
On Grace

To love and be loved is the greatest aspect of the human experience. When we find souls who see us, nurture us, and want to protect the goodness inside of us, we have found wealth beyond measure in this life. Yet the immutable truth of all human beings is that we are flawed. Thus, no relationship operating in the plane of true honesty is free from pain. This is the nature of one imperfect being relating to another. Trust becomes the cornerstone of this energetic exchange and is what sustains the bond. This trust flourishes when aligned with intuition because love does not oppose intuition; rather, love works in harmony with it and is guided by its wisdom.

Because of the inevitability of mutual pain and injury due to the imperfect nature of the beings in this bond, grace necessarily becomes central as well. Grace is the tangible expression of love; it releases others from a trial by judge and jury, centering instead their humanity. It turns off the scoreboard and recalls that there is a soul that is living life on this earth for the very first time.

We come to learn that the wounded self cannot grant grace because its sole focus is survival. It has not yet found enough safety within to stand firmly rooted in connection with another. It does not yet believe it is worthy of love and retreats at every perceived threat. To truly grant grace, we must first learn to deeply love ourselves. Creating a safe, nurturing space within reassures our psyche that we are indeed worthy of love. This inner stability allows us to trust ourselves and, in turn, trust others.

Grace honors the unspoken fears we all carry- those we may wrestle with until our final days. Grace says, *"I see you trying." "I am rooting for you."* It embodies the remembrance that we ourselves have faltered and will falter again. Because we are human and that is part of our experience here on earth. This is the embodiment of humility, which deepens trust, and communicates to our loved ones that they are safe with us. When we extend grace, we consciously override our ego's desire for rightness, allowing ourselves to expand into the full capacity of our humanity. And because grace can only be extended outward from a being that has learned to offer it inward, it serves as the empirical manifestation of a soul that believes it is worthy of the same kind of love it so freely gives.

PEDESTALS

When we struggle to express needs—either from fear of rejection or learned patterns—we tend to also unconsciously overestimate the capacity of others to intuitively meet those needs. This can cause us to place people on pedestals, where we subconsciously hope that they will take responsibility for our emotional well-being. In this dynamic, the person on the pedestal can only fall, setting up our relationships for conflict. It also reinforces in our minds that our needs are not important—or as important as theirs—leading to low self-esteem and self-resentment. To break this cycle, we must be willing to explicitly express our needs—without fear of being "too much" or of whom we might lose as a result. Your needs are inherently valid because they are *yours*, and you *need them*. And the people who love you want to meet them.

Expressing our needs does not guarantee that they will be met by others, but it does guarantee that we are meeting a core need for ourselves every time we do it.

RELATIONSHIP RULE #3

See the Good in Others, but Let Intuition Guide Alignment

One of the greatest shifts in perspective we can make is learning to see and appreciate the good in others without feeling obligated to build a relationship with them. Too often, we confuse admiration with alignment, assuming that recognizing someone's positive qualities means they are meant to play a role in our lives. Conversely, sometimes we also confuse acknowledging someone's good qualities as a wholesale endorsement of their person. But appreciation does not require attachment. It is possible to acknowledge another person's humor, intelligence, or warmth while also understanding that their presence may not be what is best for our own well-being. This distinction allows us to move through life with both openness and discernment—releasing the pressure to force relationships where they do not naturally fit. And allows us to simply enjoy experiencing life and other people.

The key to this balance lies in our own internal state of self-worth and security. When we seek love *from* others rather than *with* them, our interactions become transactional—driven by subconscious agendas rather than neutral engagement or appreciation. We may cling to those who show us glimpses of goodness, mistaking a single virtue for deep compatibility. But when we cultivate love within ourselves first, we gain the clarity to appreciate people as they are, without needing them to be anything more to us. This shift not only frees us from misplaced expectations but also allows us to build relationships with those who truly align with our values and emotional needs.

The truest nature of our intuition was not meant to pass harsh judgment or rejection; it has only ever been concerned with recognizing resonance. A person can be kind, talented, or even inspiring and have misaligned values to ours. When we refine our ability to see goodness without grasping for connection, we approach relationships with more ease, grace, and honesty. Life feels lighter and we preserve space for the relationships that are deeply right for us.

STEADY STATE

Learn to feel comfort in connection rather than attachment. Connection is about *being present and in tune* with others, where your thoughts and emotions feel steady and aligned. It is a state of steady relational consistency- where our feelings and thoughts are rooted in grounded alignment. Whereas attachment is a wanting grip that often represents a part of our identities we feel we need to keep, either from ego or from a self-love deficit. Connection is not dependent on the person, thing, or relationship remaining the same for it to make sense. Attachment however does often require that nothing changes because of the role in upholding whatever aspect of our identities it relates to. This is why "healthy attachment" *is precisely* a state of balanced connection that comes from a steadiness within oneself. So in all your pursuits and engagements, be willing to ask yourself, "Is this coming from a place of deep alignment or from a need to fill a place where I feel lack?" That is not to say that all identity pursuits should be—or even *can be*—abandoned but intentional awareness keeps the pieces of your life in perspective. This helps you hold on to the right things—and let go when you need to.

FROM A STUDIO IN OAKLAND CALIFORNIA

Affirmation

I intend to feel comfort in connection rather than attachment. I choose to be present and in tune with others while remaining rooted in grounded alignment within myself. I release the wanting grip of attachment—the belief that I need this person or thing to be whole. I allow myself to feel safe in connections that shift and evolve over time. I release what no longer serves my highest good. In all my engagements, I will ask: "Is this coming from deep alignment, or from a need to fill a place where I feel lack?" I do not shame myself for desiring or aspiring. I will remain aware so I can hold the pieces of my life in perspective and stay true to my higher self.

RELATIONSHIP RULE #4
Nothing that Is Meant for You Will Leave You Empty

In life, there is always an exchange of energy occurring in absolutely everything we choose to engage with—whether a job, a pursuit, or a relationship. The timelines of our lives unfold through the way we move in and out of these experiences.

Because the universe requires balance, any frequency that endlessly consumes you without a reciprocal replenishment is not of the natural order. When you give yourself to something—whether through time, effort, or love—it should, in some way, give back to you. Not necessarily in the way you have given or even in the way you expect, but always in a way that affirms your soul, or feeds and grows you in some way.

This is not to say that love, work, or purpose will always feel easy. In fact, the things you are most destined for will stretch you, challenge you, even break you open. But even in those breaking moments, they will never leave you spiritually depleted. Or take without offering something in return—be it wisdom, expansion, or a deeper understanding of yourself.

If something leaves you feeling perpetually empty, if it asks for your energy without ever returning it in a meaningful way, this is your sign that it is intrinsically not aligned with you. It does not make it bad or evil, just *unaligned*. When we begin to honor this truth, we stop chasing things that are not meant for us. The things that require us to continually generate new energy for its sustenance and our own. Because what is truly for us must, *by virtue of the trueness of that quality,* sustain us as well.

GROUNDED

Resist the urge to climb into anyone else's tornado. At first it's a ride but then you become lost in the storm—spinning in winds that do not belong to you. Instead of the high winds, choose what brings you peace; what feels like a sturdy home that you can rest inside of. Choose consistency and honesty. The healthy attachments that feel like a slow wood-burning fireplace. Something classic and dignified. Something substantiative. These calm horizons exist but for this, my love, you will need patience and discipline—to hold still in the shelter when the skies start to change.

COMING HOME
On Love

I'm not sure that knowing love has to be so complicated. The warmth of a fire on a cold day never feels indifferent. The comfort of our favorite blanket does not require us to be anything else to receive it. The sunlight through the rafters does not choose whom to shine upon. And our favorite sweater never feels aloof. The roof above our head doesn't change shape based on the weather. And the walls around us never ask of our deservedness to be enclosed by them. The warm shower is not keeping score of how often it warms us. And the window does not decide which days we can look through it to see the beauty outside. Our front door does not ask for conditions for its protection. And our bed never requires any proof of worthiness before we can rest in it. Yeah, I'm not sure how we made love so complicated. It seems like it really is that graspable. Like coming home.

ENIA OAKS

LOVE FEELS LIKE

A silent Saturday afternoon
the only sounds the quiet, distant hum of cars
and rustling of leaves in the trees.
The sun is dancing through the drapes,
giving the only source of light,
a playful, romantic one.
We are the only two in this world.
Exploring,
with gratitude,
and trust,
and it is just
easy.

RELATIONSHIP RULE #5
Just Because You Feel It Strongly Does Not Make it True

Some feelings arrive like tsunamis—overwhelming, absolute, and convincing. They flood the mind with such intensity that it seems as though their presence alone is proof of their truth. However, recognizing that emotions themselves cannot be facts, but rather are *responses to perception*, allows us to better navigate through them. When something happens, it is important to recognize that our perception of it is shaped by *our past, our fears, and our subconscious narratives*. The emotions we feel are then *a response* to this perception. They arise from conditioning, from unhealed wounds, and from interpretations shaped by experience and projections rather than reality itself. This opens the door to cognitive distortion, emotional reasoning, in which we equate our strong feeling with facts.

Emotional reasoning, unlike our intuition, is very loud. Intuition does not shout, it does not spiral, and it does not overwhelm. It does not arrive in the form of racing thoughts or panic. Instead it is a quiet knowing, a stillness beneath the noise. Emotional reasoning is urgent, demanding, desperate for certainty. More than that it desperately and immediately needs to be acted upon to alleviate the discomfort it brings. Intuition is subtle, patient, persistent. Where emotion clouds perception, intuition clarifies it. Where emotion reacts, intuition quietly knows.

If you grew up in unpredictable environments, emotional intensity may have developed as a survival mechanism--a way to detect threat before it arrives. But this sensitivity, if unchecked, can lead to seeking out evidence for and believing rejection where none exists, seeing malice where there is only indifference, and assuming failure where growth is still unfolding.

The antidote to this is not suppression—it is awareness and the infusion of *time*. It is learning to pause between feeling and action; and between feeling and conclusion. To ask, "*What else could be true?* " To recognize that emotions deserve to be felt but not always followed. Sometimes an emotion *is* in tandem step with your intuition, and other times, with just a bit of time, you see that it is actually your fears shouting from the shadows.

FROM A STUDIO IN OAKLAND CALIFORNIA

TEN FEET TALL

Love is not necessarily
the burning passion of chaotic encounters,
but it is always
the emotional safety of a soul
who wants to protect your deepest well-being.

It is not necessarily
grand prophetic gestures,
but it is always
emotional follow-through and consistency.

It is not necessarily
different than anything you've ever known,
but it is always
somewhere that feels like home—
where you seem to just fit.

It is not necessarily
understanding your pain,
but it is always
making space for it.

ENIA OAKS

It is not necessarily
finding someone so good
you feel like you have to become bigger
just to meet them at that level;
but it is always
finding someone
who sees you
in a way
that makes you feel like
the tallest,
most beautiful version
of *yourself.*

RELATIONSHIP RULE #6:
Remain in the Present Moment with Every Connection

The pain we feel when a relationship ends is proportional to the degree to which we dreamt of its foreverness. Similarly, the pain we *cause* in a relationship is proportional to the degree to which we relived the past through it. This is probably one of the most difficult aspects of being with another person: our timelines may meet in the present, but this does not guarantee that our hearts are in the same realm.

When the present feels too painful, we sometimes try to grasp for certainty and escape by either dwelling in the past or trying to fast-forward into the future. We may try to outrun our fears by forcefully molding our daydreams into our present reality; in this case we give *too much too soon*, hoping that our effort will secure something, *anything*. When we dwell too much in the past, we give too little, believing that each step must be carefully calculated to avoid being hurt again. We, in essence, anchor ourselves to the last versions of ourselves that felt in control.

But love cannot be built on projections—it can only be built on presence. *In the present.* It can neither be preserved through over-giving, nor protected through withholding. Only time can reveal what a new connection has in store. And there is no amount of over-performing that will make something that is not meant for you to stay. The more you over-invest, the more you attached you become. Similarly, there is no amount of cutting open of the other person that will reveal how it all will end. And the more you attempt to do so, the more likely you will sabotage something that could have been beautiful.

To stay present in any new connection, we must be willing to be honest with ourselves about the state of our hearts in the present. Knowing where we are allows us to temper ourselves—so that we meet each connection for what it is, not what we hope or fear it will become. Love is not a problem to be solved—it is an experience to be lived, fully, in the only place it can ever exist: the present.

So be vulnerable enough to allow your actions to reflect your feelings, but patient enough to show and give only in proportion to the present reality. Trust that love unfolds in its own time, and that what is real does not need to be forced or rushed.

What is meant for you will reach for you just as you reach for it.

FROM A STUDIO IN OAKLAND CALIFORNIA

A LOVE LETTER TO THE ANXIOUS HEART

You are so deeply worthy of a love that feels like home—the kind that wraps around you with certainty, the kind that makes you exhale and confirms what you've dreamed of does exist. It has always existed. And you, with your wide-open heart, were never wrong to believe in it.

The way you love is beautiful. It's rare. It's magic. You see people in ways they've never been seen before. In ways they been *longing* to be seen. You give warmth without hesitation, you pour deeply, you love fully. That is a gift and one of the most divine expressions of humanity. But here's what I need you to understand: that love—your magic—belongs to you first. Before anyone else, before anything else, it *has to* be for you. That kind of warmth, thoughtfulness, affection, support, devotion you express in love must be directed toward yourself first. Why? Because when you begin to give to yourself first, something extraordinary happens: your magic magnifies. Your aura magnifies. And you become so accustomed to being loved *intentionally*, it soothes your soul so deeply that anyone who does not meet you in that intention will be unable to remain.

Somewhere along the way, you learned to believe the most destructive lie told by our fears: that love must be proven, earned, or chased. And the thing is, there are people who will see your magic—your exquisite heart—and try to hoard it for themselves, meanwhile convincing you that it actually belongs to them. Before you've realized it, they have distorted reality—making you believe that *they* are the source of your light; that it is *them* who owns your magic. You will chase after them, believing you need them. Begging for a bit of what already belongs to you entirely. Because that love and beauty you thought you saw in them—felt with them—was actually radiating from inside of you *onto* them.

The truth is that your most beautiful love story will be with someone who shares a bit of their magic with you as well. You will never have to chase them for it. Rather, the two of you will create an overflowing well to bask in together. And that person? They are looking for you, too. But they will only recognize you once you have reclaimed full ownership of your magic— living in and wearing it proudly. That is the beacon that will lead them to you

FROM A STUDIO IN OAKLAND CALIFORNIA

ON REJECTION

The idea and experience of rejection as we know it is often one that is anchored by a premature attachment to something or someone, or an unrealized need for control. What we don't understand is that we may be unwittingly attaching ourselves to things that may destroy, demoralize, or derail us. When we understand that the things we attract in our lives appear once we meet them on the same frequency, we begin to better understand the experience of life. Subsequently, we understand that what doesn't meet us was not meant for us at that given point in our lives. And there is likely a divine purpose in that misalignment. This does not mean that some of these experiences will not be disappointing. We are human after all. However, just know that what is truly aligned with the core of your being is reaching for you just as you are reaching for it.

Through this lens we see that rejection is a necessary part of life that works to mold and redirect our lives to the spaces that are truly meant for us. The spaces that *want* us. If we can learn to grant rejection a necessary role in our lives and honor it as a trusted ally and guide, we can more quickly find our best and most honorable lives.

RELATIONSHIP RULE #7
Love Must Be Chosen

There is a version of love sold to us in palatable bites, where it is a passion-fueled feeling. In that version, the feeling *is* the point. However, this is the smallest conceptualization of one of the most profound experiences of our human existence. Yes, love is felt but it also requires that we consciously choose it—in practice, in action, in words.

The truth is that the feeling of love only serves as a heartbeat in the center of the experience. The actual structure of the *heart that is beating* is made up of our choices in relation to it. Just as we can strengthen the heart through presence and care, we can also stifle it through neglect or fear. Therefore, love is never is just something that *happens* to us—it is something we actively and tangibly create. Something we choose. That rush of chemistry or the serendipity of two souls crossing paths only tell us, *maybe here*. But love, real love, will ask for something deeper. It will ask for willingness. And presence. It will ask us to step beyond the fleeting emotions and into something purposeful, something intended.

Loving in this way with intention and purpose will stretch you. Because it needs to. It will show you the parts of yourself that are still learning how to be open, how to trust, how to remain steady in connection with another soul. But that stretching is for your becoming. Each time we lean into this version of love, we are stretching our own capacity to receive that same kind of love—or a greater one—in return. We evolve out of the narrow, vision of it—where it is merely a feeling—to the grand, energy-multiplying reality of it where our souls are reflected back to us in their most exquisite form. And even when a story does not last in the form we hoped, the new expanded being that we inhabit as a result of having participated affirms that it was never wasted. That kind of powerful being-expanding experience cannot just *happen* to us, rather we must choose it.

When we understand this truth about love, we stop prioritizing its highs and lows and instead, learn to seek and assess it with purpose. The experience of it becomes an extension of our larger becoming where we are learning not just to feel the emotion, but to also choose the meaning of it. A meaning rooted in our humanity that we can then practice with intention.

ME AND YOU

You can have both—yourself and your relationships. But protecting both will require setting boundaries that honor your individuality and also allow space for connection. Too often, we believe it needs to be one or the other—that to love fully means to sacrifice ourselves, or that to preserve ourselves means to keep others at a distance. Neither of these are true.

True authenticity and our happiest lives do not require we choose between solitude and connection; rather, they ask of us to integrate both. Maintaining a strong sense of self is not at odds with deep connection with another—it is what makes love sustainable. It is possible to soften into another, to merge your life with theirs, without dissolving into them. Love is not meant to consume; it is meant to expand—to make room for both souls to exist fully, side by side.

LOVE YOU, *FREELY*

At its core, love is freedom. It is the recognition and support of another person's humanity to evolve into their authentic life journey. It is the willingness to accept that sometimes the evolution may mean that the two paths diverge, which also means a commitment to remaining grounded and stable within yourself. It is the allowing of another soul to choose yours, and to choose the life you will share together as part of their life story. Yes, love is choice, intention, and commitment. But is also truth, individuality, and release.

RELATIONSHIP RULE #8:
Examine Your Resentments, Find Your Core Needs

Resentment is the natural byproduct of unmet needs, therefore your resentments offer valuable insight into what you need to feel safe and loved in relationships.

If you repeatedly find yourself feeling uncared for across multiple relationships, this may indicate a difficulty in expressing, advocating for, or defending your needs. Over time, your inner being—the part of you that longs for love and protection—begins to harbor resentment toward both you and others. It resents you for failing to protect it, which manifests as low self-esteem. And it resents others, sometimes before they've even had the chance to show up for you, because it has already decided that disappointment is inevitable.

To break this cycle, you must be willing to explicitly express your needs, without fear of being "too much" or of who you might lose as a result. This act alone sends a powerful message to your being: your needs matter, and you are worthy of them being taken seriously. From there, you must be willing to establish and uphold boundaries when those needs are not met.

Because here's the truth: some people will feel the need to reduce you to their understanding of what you *should* be like. And with that, they will reduce the amount of need you are allowed to have. They'll either intentionally ignore the realities of your person, or their limited perspective will simply not comprehend it. You will be a trigger of cognitive dissonance because in order for them to feel safe in *how they understand themselves*, they need you to occupy a *very* specific space in their reality. Do not become discouraged or disheartened by this. It is not your cross to bear. This limited version of you exists only in their mind and has no weight or bearing on the fullness of your actual person. Your only task is to identify where you are continuously left wanting and hungry. Come to know these tender areas because they are your most core of needs.

Then you make a point to honor these needs without apology. The more you do this, the more you reclaim your right to be seen fully—whether specific people choose to or not. With time and practice, this will erode patterns of resentment, as your needs become more consistently acknowledged and fulfilled.

ENIA OAKS

LOVE SAYS

When you are upset, I know that means you need more love.
I know these are your favorite, so I bought a dozen more.
You can do this—just take it step by step.
Will you dance with me? Here, I'll show you how.
You are wonderful. Just as you are.
I did not mean to hurt you. I'm sorry.
What do you think? I made this for you.
I believe in you. What do you need?
You look tired. Have you eaten?
When your shoulders go up, I know that means you need a hug.
That looks heavy. Let me help you carry it.
Tell me everything. I'm listening.
Rest here, I've got you.
Welcome home.

RELATIONSHIP RULE #9:
How a Person Feels About Themself Is How They Will Treat You

Here is a simple truth we often overlook in relationships: people do not make exceptions to their nature. How someone moves through the world—their kindness or cruelty, their generosity or selfishness—is a direct reflection of their internal world. And no matter how special we believe we are to them, we are not immune to the way they fundamentally operate.

At the core of this rule is their self-perception. The way we are to others is the only way we know how to be to ourselves, to anyone. People who move with grace and compassion toward others are often those who have learned grace and compassion for themselves. Similarly, those who habitually demean, exploit, or dismiss others are rarely in a place of deep self-respect. Their external actions mirror their internal conditions.

It's easy to believe we will be the exception, particularly when we experience the most well-intentioned version of them. We convince ourselves that somehow, this person who gossips about others, lashes out, or withdraws in moments of tension will not do the same to us. That if they love us enough, they will treat us differently. But love does not override a person's operating system—it merely places us inside of it.

If someone lacks integrity with others, they will eventually lack integrity with you.

If someone is emotionally unavailable to the world, they will not be emotionally available to you.

If someone speaks with contempt about others, they will one day speak with contempt about you.

A person cannot give from an emotional reserve they do not have. If they have not practiced self-awareness, self-kindness, and a sense of accountability within themselves, they will not suddenly acquire those traits in their relationship with you.

If you want to build a relationship rooted in respect, depth, and kindness, you must choose people who move through the world with those values—not just toward you, but toward everyone. Character is consistent and does not make exceptions.

We cannot change this fact by loving them harder. And we cannot rewrite someone's self-perception by believing in their potential. We simply bear witness to what already exists.

FOR ME
On Forgiveness

Forgiveness is not understanding.
And it is not accepting responsibility for another's misdeeds.
It is rejecting a projection of unworthiness that was cast upon you.
It is not weakness.
Rather, it is proof of an indomitable spirit.
It is not defeat or surrender.
It is standing up with your head high and reclaiming your power.
It is *not necessarily* grace for another.
But it is *always* grace for yourself.
It is an allowing of your own wholeness once again.
Forgiveness is not granting absolution. It is release.
It does not require accepting someone back into your life.
You are allowed to forgive someone and never speak to them again.
It does not mean you are doomed to repeat an experience.
That wisdom is yours forever.
Forgiveness is not naïve.
Rather it is the highest form of wisdom.
It is the recognition that anything that binds your soul in this life
is a prison you inhabit alone.
Forgiveness recognizes that holding malice does not bring
retribution or settle the score.
It only entraps you in a futile stupor.
You see, the point of forgiveness has absolutely nothing to do with
a single other person.
It is a revolutionary act of self-liberation.

ENIA OAKS

THE JOURNEY OF LIFE

FROM A STUDIO IN OAKLAND CALIFORNIA

AND MY SOUL SAID TO ME:
"YOU SAID WE'D ALWAYS BE FREE"

Did we do it? The thing we always said we would.
Did we go? *How was it?*
That time we said it would be the last time, *was it?*
What about that job?
You know the one, that made us feel like we were suffocating,
did we leave it?
Did we ever make peace with Mom?
I know, I know.
What about Dad?
That's okay.
Did we ever let ourselves fall?
You know, in love.
And?
Was it the good stuff, like we said we'd hold out for?
Do we still believe in the goodness of the universe?
What about mankind?
What about God?
Do we still laugh?
Often?
Did we ever save ourselves, like we said we would?
That thing we don't talk about, *are we okay now?*
Did we find our truth?
How about what makes us feel alive? Did we ever find that?
Did we ever let go?
Completely?

ENIA OAKS

FROM A STUDIO IN OAKLAND CALIFORNIA

THE JOURNEY OF LIFE

You do not need to have life figured out—not now, not at any point in the future where you might find yourself feeling lost. This is the biggest secret the world keeps hidden: no one alive has figured out life, they have just learned how to live—how to keep moving forward. Every single person who has built something beautiful or great could not have planned for the full enormity of it. But they understood something key: how they showed up mattered more than any perfect plan. You see, this is the magic variable in absolutely everything—*the energy you bring*. When you commit to showing up as your best self, it is inevitable that you will grow—either into the person capable of achieving a given desire, or into a person that will find another, more aligned path entirely. So take a deep breath, and take your next step with conviction and courage. What is meant for you will surely find you, so long as you keep moving forward.

WHAT CALLS YOU

Take notice of the experiences that feel not just aligned, but like they are calling you. There is likely something key you are meant to experience through them or some way you are meant to be transformed inside of them. You always have the choice to decide in which ways you want to be stretched and any time, you can decide that you no longer want to explore or participate in a certain facet of life. And that is okay. But take notice of these experiences nonetheless. They undoubtedly contain vital information about some element of existence your soul craves. That could be a certain degree of intensity, a certain exploration of your capacity, or an important satiation of your curiosity that is necessary for you to truly understand what it is you need in your life. Even if the experience does not lead where you expected, it will still bring you closer to yourself. Each of these paths you walk, no matter for how long, offers you a piece of the map that guides you home—a home built from the inside out.

FROM A STUDIO IN OAKLAND CALIFORNIA

THERE IS ONLY ALIGNMENT AND MISALIGNMENT

Life — in all its noise and complexity — really does tend to sort itself along that line. So if you don't know what to do next, look for alignment. Ask yourself the consequential questions. What do you believe in? What do you hope for? What do you feel so convicted about you feel it deeply in your bones? What refuses to be ignored? What lessons have you learned and will absolutely never repeat again? How do you envision the world, and what role do you want to play in it? What makes life feel beautiful? What fills you with a sense of honor and purpose? And most importantly, what will bring you closer to the person you are meant to become?

These are the questions that point you home.

CALM

It is normal to feel overwhelmed by life some days, or many days. Our psyches were not made for constant stimulation, expectations of immediacy, and ever-present social connection. When you feel overwhelmed in this kind of environment it actually means that your inner being has still maintained its memory of a calmer state. It is making a bid for you to take a moment to slow down and just be. It is attempting to capture that state of serenity so that it can feel safe once again. It is asking for you to take several long deep breaths in and just feel stillness around you. To set down all that pulls at your attention, close your eyes, and feel your heartbeat. Feel your humanness without any demands. Go outside, allow the fresh air in, and feel the sun on your skin. It just needs to know that you are still able to feel the ground underneath your feet. It needs to remember for one moment, what it feels like to just be.

FROM A STUDIO IN OAKLAND CALIFORNIA

SALVE

Allow periods of your life to be a salve for your existence.
Let them heal what needs to be healed,
replenish what has been consumed,
and release what needs to leave you.
But do not make a home inside of salve.
It was never meant to house you,
only to ready you for what comes next.
For this place of healing is a place of passage, not a destination.
So let it tend to you, and once renewed,
Carry on your hero's journey.

GOOD FOR THE SOUL

Exploration is good for the soul
Failure is good for the soul
Rejection is good for the soul
Heartbreak is good for the soul
Laughter is good for the soul
Forgiveness is good for the soul
Mistakes are good for the soul
Joy is good for the soul
Creation is good for the soul
Sunshine is good for the soul
Water is good for the soul
Grief is good for the soul
Pain is good for the soul
Sacrifice is good for the soul
Struggle is good for the soul
Loss is good for the soul
Love is good for the soul
Connection is good for the soul
Believing in something bigger than yourself is good for the soul

SPRINGTIME

Those who are willing to start over when life takes them to places they find undignified or unaligned with their highest self are the most remarkable and honest of souls. These people are limitless because they have discovered a superpower: the belief in and willingness to trust in their own agency. They understand that honoring your soul is the foundation of true inner strength. And that when you are willing to declare the space that you will occupy in this world, the universe shifts the details of your reality to mold around that space. These people move through life with an acceptance that many of life's experiences are meant to be temporary and that sometimes, *often times*, it is up to you to move on and start again.

ENIA OAKS

I *AM* HOME

They look at you with foreign eyes,
as if you belong nowhere.
As if they are not foreign to you, as well.
As if we are all not out of place *somewhere*.
They say this land isn't of your ancestors—
but is this earth collectively not ours?
Mankind has a way of gutting one another.
We know this.
Do they?
The journey here was constructed from hope for a new start.
A hope to build a new home.
Here? Not quite right.
There? the features do not fit.
Your people *are* beautiful.
You never realized that was up for debate.
Your name echoes through generations before you.
Your mother was intentional about that.
They say your dad's accent is hard to understand,
but you've never missed a single word he's said.
They imply you don't deserve dignity,
But I don't think they know that it's not up to them to decide.
The richness coursing through your veins
doesn't require an endorsement.
You've tried to make it fit, *I know you have.*
But I don't think it was meant to.

FROM A STUDIO IN OAKLAND CALIFORNIA

I think we were always supposed to be neighbors—
bonded by our common humanity,
but *different,* because *that* is beautiful.
I think you were always supposed to just be *you*.
I've met some other "misfits" here,
and my god, they are the kind of exquisite you write stories about.
I don't think we are in bad company at all.

METAMORPHOSIS

We humans were never meant to remain the same throughout our lives, or even through a sequence of years. The tricky part is that we have to be willing to adapt and update our movements and routines for the people we are becoming—step by step. Evolution demands that we shed versions of ourselves that once felt like home, leaving behind familiar comforts for the unknown. And this shedding happens over and over and over again. It requires courage to embrace the discomfort of transition, to accept that what once served us may no longer fit. But this is the essence of transformation: to honor who we were, make space for where we are currently, and set plans and routines for who we are becoming—who we are meant to be. And to trust that each evolution brings us closer to a truer, fuller existence. One where we have wings.

FROM A STUDIO IN OAKLAND CALIFORNIA

WHEN THE SKY SPLITS OPEN

There will be moments you never see coming—when the world as you know it ends. It won't announce itself. And there will be no warning, no time to prepare. One day, you are whole, believing in the goodness of life. And then, in the next, something happens—something so unexpected, so earth-shattering—that it leaves a crack in your foundation, a wound that will never quite close the same way again.

When we are young, our understanding of the world is shaped by the messaging provided by caretakers, our environment, our inner beings, and the limited rationalizations of our own experiences. We are taught the golden rule: to do unto others as you would have done to you. We see protagonists communicate vulnerability and humanity. Justice wins, and good triumphs over evil. Fairness is important. Even when *we* experience harshness, our minds filter it through the lens of a soul that is innocent. So we are still able to believe in goodness because we *are* goodness. We live from the inside out, relating to the world from our understanding of how it is supposed to be.

And then, the sky splits open.

It could be the death of someone you love. The betrayal of a friend you trusted with everything. The realization that those you looked up to were not who they pretended to be. It could be the slow erosion of hope, chipped away by disappointments that begin to stack like heavy stones in your chest. It could be one moment, one conversation, or a hundred small instances that eventually collapse under their own weight. Whatever it is, it leaves you staring at the sky, wondering what the suffering is supposed to mean and when it will end.

These are the moments that change everything. Because once you have seen the dark side of existence, you can no longer unsee it. You are always now aware of its presence. The illusions of fairness and order crumble, and the reality of life—the messy, unjust, often brutal nature of it—stands stark and unyielding before you. You realize that justice does not always prevail, that goodness does not always shield you, and that pain does not always come with a lesson tied neatly in a bow.

In these moments, choice arises. Some turn away from this realization, retreating into disillusionment, shutting themselves off from the parts of the world that once felt warm and promising. This is the only way they know how to give their souls salvation. Others—perhaps the ones who suffer the deepest, who lose the most—find themselves forced into an expansion they did not ask for. They are broken open, hollowed out by the kind of grief that demands a reckoning. And within that emptiness—that *need for justice*—something new begins to form. A different kind of belief. One that is no longer naive, but deliberate. One that does not ignore the dark, but insists on creating light despite it.

This is conscious reclamation of lost idealism. The result of an understanding that, while you cannot change the entire world, you *can* impact the parts of it that you touch. And that in order for goodness to exist, there have to be people willing to live it and put it out into the world. You will see that you can choose kindness, because it is an affirmation of the world *you* want to live in. You can choose love as a testament to the depth of your own humanity. You can choose to create something beautiful not as a form of denial, but as a declaration that light still belongs here. You can choose to be your own proof of the goodness that your soul needs to know exists in the world.

We will carry our wounds with us—some for a lifetime. But we also carry something else: the choice of what we do with that weight. Whether we let it pull us under, or whether we use it to carve a path forward, one that others might follow. One that heals our spirit *from the inside out.*

The sky will split open many times in a lifetime. You will be broken, again and again. But each time, you will also be given the chance to rebuild. To choose, despite everything, to keep believing in something worth saving.

THE FUNDAMENTAL QUESTION

It becomes evident to us all as we progress through life that there is one questions that matters above all others.
And that is,
Who is it that I want to become?
For within that answer lies the reason for existence.

FROM A STUDIO IN OAKLAND CALIFORNIA

HAND MADE

Your intuition, at its core, is wired for survival, familiarity, resonance, and above all, safety. Though beautiful and most well intended, if left unchallenged, it will mistake playing small for security and worthwhile risk for danger. But your intuition was never meant to keep you small; it was meant to evolve with you. To expand its range, however, you have to consciously shape it to feel comfort amidst the unknown. You have to deliberately introduce it to new landscapes, teach it that uncertainty does not always mean danger, and that discomfort does not always mean you should turn back. Just like clay, you have to intentionally create imprints and indents where you want it to have the capacity to hold a new shape or form. And when you begin to recondition it to recognize adventure as safe, to see risk as a doorway or opportunity rather than a threat, something powerful inside of you shifts. Instead of your intuition seeking only what you have known, it will take on its most realized form as your brave inner guide leading you through your most breathtaking life.

ENIA OAKS

WHY NOT ME?

When you learn to start asking, "Why not me?",
life begins to open
in more beautiful ways than you could have ever imagined.
Because the truth is,
Why not you?

FROM A STUDIO IN OAKLAND CALIFORNIA

GOOD FEAR

Today I cried.
sitting by the window, watching the five tall palms sway steadily outside.
I didn't know there was this much in there to let out.
I guess it had been a while.
I'm not completely sure exactly why I'm crying.
If I really think about it, there's a lot I've been holding in.
When I look up at the sky, I feel like I'm six again.
It stretches on forever.
I've always liked thinking about that.
I like the idea that the world is so big.
I feel a lot of fear these days,
But I think it's the good kind of fear.
Like when I was learning how to ride my rollerblades for the first time.
"It's good to be brave," I remember my dad would say.

THE CHOICE

You always have a choice in how you pursue meaning in this life. But know that there are some paths that leave you restless, empty, and always chasing. While others allow you to move through life with a sense of purpose, depth, and connection. Any pursuit rooted in a desire to stand on top of—rather than beside--other people will *invariably* lead to your own undoing. If there is not an intrinsic curiosity or personal fulfilment in the thing itself, even if you reach the peak, you will find a hollow darkness where you thought triumph would be. The kind of darkness that makes you existentially wonder *"is this is all there is to life?"* The truth is that power, when sought for its own sake, does not nourish. It only devours. Contrary to what misguided narratives may say, life is *not* a zero-sum game. The life that feels the most beautiful and worth living is the one where abundance pours from upholding others, rather than trampling them. It is the life not built through dominance, but rather through contribution. True success is not about standing above. It is about building something meaningful with others that lasts.

FROM A STUDIO IN OAKLAND CALIFORNIA

BECOMING

Becoming the person you want to be will have to be an intentional process. At any given point in time, there are a million different pressures and forces molding your psyche from all different sides. So if you do not take control of this process, your person will be created by the circumstances of your life. First, you define who it is you want to be. Then go through that list with intention. If you want to become more confident, seek experiences that require you to use your voice. If you want to become more charismatic, learn *how* to like other people. If you want to become wiser, practice being more reflective and self-examining. If you want to become more self-assured, look for challenges that will stretch you. If you want to learn to discern between your anxiety and your intuition, focus on becoming more patient. Learn to sit with uncertainty and allow clarity to emerge before you act. If you want to feel overall happier in your life, practice shifting your perspective more often into one of gratitude. Who you become is not a matter of fate, but of choice—whether you realize you are choosing or not. And every choice you make is a step toward or away from your truest, most fulfilled, self. Toward or away from your biggest life.

One of the most beautiful things about life is the fact that every single experience you have layers onto all the others. No event—big or small—is ever insignificant in the grand picture: in your becoming. Oftentimes, the profoundness of a given moment can only be appreciated at some point down the line. The reality is that there is no shortcut to a big life. There are many shortcuts to a life that *looks* big but is killing you on the inside of it. But the kind of big that feeds you as you feed it can only be created organically piece by piece, *layer by layer*. The truth is that, if this kind of reality was easy to come by or fake, many more people would have achieved it. Instead, the *layers* are the recipe—the vital ingredients. They are the containers where the molding and evolution of your being occur. Where you become someone who can actually hold what you say you desire. These layers cannot be faked if they are to create the potency within you.

So be intentional about these steps. Seek and appreciate the fact that life always gives us the option for growth and expansion if we choose it. Allow the journey through these layers to create the footprint roadmap to the person and life you desire. Because the grandest existence is the one that is true in all of its layers.

FROM A STUDIO IN OAKLAND CALIFORNIA

ON: PURPOSE

I think one thing we get wrong about the idea of purpose is that it has to be this singular grand pursuit in life. That it is meant to be the existential culmination of the most realized parts of our souls. It *is* that, but I also think that definition puts a lot of pressure on it. Most simply, purpose just seems to be, *what you do you believe in and are willing to put intention toward*? Purpose can be the way you call your mom regularly so she never feels forgotten or unimportant. Or the way you work so hard so your family can feel beauty and goodness in this life. It is in the way you always smile at babies so they can always experience light in their world. Or the way you choose to treat everyone you meet with the same respect no matter their circumstances in life, because that's just the way it should be. I don't think purpose has to be so complex. It can just be your commitment to embodying the values you strongly believe in.

At its core, I think purpose is some kind of confirmation to the self. A confirmation of what life should be like, a confirmation of your capabilities, a confirmation of your deepest beliefs, a confirmation of love. It is the way we replant our deepest wounds into something beautiful. The connection between our inspiration and deepest layers of fulfilment. We often talk about purpose as something to chase or figure out, but it seems more true to me that it is something we instead have to learn to recognize within the best parts of *ourselves*.

ENIA OAKS

THE SUM OF A LIFE FULLY LIVED

This is approximately 27lbs. of birthday cake, 65,000 moments of worry. It is 34,849,000 thoughts about the future, and 5 shake-you-loose-from-your-beliefs experiences. It is 350 hours of crying over heartbreak, 90 hours of staring at the ceiling, wondering if this is all there is. It is 7 times you truly thought you might break but didn't. It is 20 to 25 deeply etched wrinkles on the face and 28,950 meals with the ones we love most. It is 115 moments of pure, unfiltered joy—the kind that makes you forget yourself completely. It is 9 phone calls that changed everything. And 160 deeply uncomfortable conversations that needed to be had. It is one or two days you wish you could live all over again. It is an uncountable number of second chances. And enough failures to fill up a journal. It is as many grand adventures as you are brave enough to have.

The weight of a life is *truly and exactly* related to how fully you intend to live it.

FROM A STUDIO IN OAKLAND CALIFORNIA

YOU

I wondered
where I would find you

Here?

Then
suddenly,
like a matter of fact,
there *you* were.

-*A Poem to Self*

BEAUTY IN EXISTENCE

FROM A STUDIO IN OAKLAND CALIFORNIA

PASSING THROUGH

Life changes when you start viewing it as a series of experiences, moments you are moving through. That the exact point of it is to experience it all. From this perspective, we can understand that there aren't always reasons for the things that happen to us. Yes, sometimes, there *is* an energetic cause and effect. Other times, however, we are simply being carried along the universe's timeline. You choose certain paths and there are myriads of events, both beautiful and tragic, that can unfold from there. Down one path you may meet the love of your life and build a beautiful home filled with laughter. That same home may be hit with tragedy, but it does not change the love you felt in the midst of it. That experience is yours to keep forever. It will remain imprinted into your soul for eternity, layering to create the unique patina of a life fully lived. Of *your* life fully lived. The joy, the heartbreak, the stillness of certain moments—it all stays, each piece a part of the larger story. So aim only to experience your life as it unfolds in front of you. Let it all leave its mark. At the end of it all, the stories contained are the substantiated realities of your humanity—of your beautiful human experience.

ENIA OAKS

LOVE LETTERS FROM THE UNIVERSE

When you are running late,
and all of the traffic lights turn green.
When you are thinking about someone you love
and their name pops up on your phone.
The feeling of sunshine on your skin.
When the thing you made yourself sick worrying about
just sort of works itself out.
When that good news you had been waiting for
shows up just in time.
When a complete stranger saves the day.
That warm shower after a long rainy day.
When you exit unharmed from a situation
that should have ended much worse.
When you hear the joy and innocence of a baby's laugh.
When you suddenly find the strength
to change your life,
and your life seems to then conspire for good in response.
When someone surprises you so beautifully and thoughtfully.
When you walk off your flight
with a perfect landing
and the little girl inside of you meets eyes and smile with your female pilot.
When life leads you to the exact places and people
that heal what you did not realize what broken inside of you.

FROM A STUDIO IN OAKLAND CALIFORNIA

When the timing of everything works out
better than you could have *ever* planned for yourself.

These love letters are intimate reminders,
penned for you,
by a universe who wants you to know that
you were never forgotten.
That you are always being held in this life.

BEAUTY IN STILLNESS

There are moments in life where the world goes quiet. These are the most precious gifts, easy to overlook or take for granted. This world often tells us that we must go, and do, and strive, and achieve. But many of us have never been taught how to just be. How to sit quietly and listen to the rustle of the trees or notice the bird flying in patterns through the sky. We never learned how to observe the stillness of a quiet room. And how to just allow the experience of this stillness to be the activity of the moment. For there, beneath all the noise, we are beautifully reminded that in stillness we find the most captivating moments in existence.

Affirmation

I give myself permission to slow down. To let the quiet be enough. To sit with the rustle of leaves, the hush of silence around me, the space between thoughts. I do not have to earn my existence through movement. I am allowed to be. And in the stillness, I will hold gratitude and remember: this moment is alive with meaning, and I am already whole inside of it.

FROM A STUDIO IN OAKLAND CALIFORNIA

CINNAMON

The more you learn about life—and grow to understand it—the richer your experience of it becomes. You start to see and appreciate the world in more grounded, nuanced ways. And through that process, you begin to realize: the way to enrich your life is by learning to enrich your soul. By learning to be present through all of your senses.

Imagine: there was once a time when you didn't know the name of that warm, sweet, spicy smell drifting through the air. You'd catch it, feel a kind of comfort, but not know what you were experiencing—only that you liked it.

Of course, not knowing its name didn't make it any less beautiful. But once you *learned* to call it cinnamon, something subtle shifted. The experience deepened. It gained shape.

That's what recognition does. That's what naming does.

Once you've had experiences that teach you how to notice the beauty in your life, your experience of life becomes *that much more beautiful*. Once you learn to recognize what is, and give language to what you feel, your experience deepens in layers.

When you've known real love, and been loved well, you understand its magnitude. So when it comes again, your appreciation of it will be that much richer.

Once you have known true despair, you become profoundly grateful for your joy.

Once you've lived without, the smallest comforts feel like grace.

One by one through life's experiences, you learn to recognize honor, intention, beautiful serendipity, bravery, kindness, truth, effort, protection, growth, and justice.

You learn to recognize goodness. *Just like cinnamon.*

FROM A STUDIO IN OAKLAND CALIFORNIA

RITUALS

When you lift your mug, let the steam rise to meet you before the first sip. Allow your hands to move with intention when smoothing oil into your skin, feeling the warmth of your own touch. When the sun peeks out from behind the rain cloud, allow yourself to bask in it for a moment, letting its rays warm your skin. Allow the water from your shower head to tap down, and mentally trace the massage down your back with each drop. Wrap yourself in fabrics that drape just right and settle against your skin like a familiar, loving presence. Sip warm tea and feel the soothing feeling radiate from the inside of you outward. When you lay down at night, center your gratitude before sleep, letting the day close gently around you. As the world rushes on, you can choose to linger, stretching each moment just long enough to feel its contours.

You see, ritual is not just habit; it is a way of slowing time, of turning the ordinary into something deeply felt. When you make a practice of presence, of noticing, and of moving through life as if it were something to be savored, you transform even the simplest moments into something deeply luxurious and exquisite.

BALANCE

Do not ever forget that the universe tends toward balance and homeostasis. It requires it. All living creatures and ecosystems, the forces of nature, the tectonic plates beneath our feet, the planets in orbit, all submit to the order of balance. For every force, there is a counteracting force. If you feel an imbalance at this current moment, just wait. Hold on tight and wait. But know that the shifts are occurring in the cosmos.

ECLIPSE

Darkness is not an interruption of life, but rather a necessary phase of it. Eclipses remind us of this—that it is part of life's natural rhythm. When the sun and moon disappear in their own cycles, they always return in perfect time. These celestial bodies do not resist these moments of darkness, so why do we resist our own?

Darkness is not the absence of life, but rather it is the place where life is recalibrated. It is where illusions dissolve, truth can be heard in the quiet, and we are undressed, revealing what is real. Just like the moon in eclipse, we remain whole even when unseen. Our light is not gone, only waiting for the right moment to emerge. The mistake is in believing that we must rush through the dark, or fear its stillness. In reality, the darkness only asks of us to surrender to it, to trust it, and to let it do its quiet work. *It asks us to rest.* When we learn to nurture ourselves through these eclipses, we honor the transformational processes that allow our becoming.

So instead of fearing these moments where things go quiet and our old selves disappear, let's hold reverence for them as they are omens of evolution. When we emerge, we will do so not as we were, but as something brand new, clearer, and more aligned.

RELEASE

If the how does not yet make sense, life is asking for you to release and expand into it. When you release your most beautiful and earnest intentions into the universe, it receives them, and movements begin to occur on an energetic level. Some call this the law of attraction. Another way to look at it is that when you surrender the will of your conscious mind into a larger desire, what you are actually requesting is a desired *state of being* that can create and hold that particular desire. That state of being cannot occupy a space that is already filled. So by surrendering your will into it, you are releasing your attachments to your current state of being, and thus creating that space within yourself. You become more expanded, and a new state can now slowly start taking root. Your expanded self now has the capacity to access insights and see paths that it could not previously see because it inhabits an entirely different frame of reference—one that has the willingness to operate on an energetic rather than physical plane. And as a result, it moves forward through guidance of its energy.

SERENDIPITY AND US

Serendipity happens from the collision of millions of individual possibilities available in any given space and time. And all success is related to serendipity—which is made up of space and time—plus state of mind. The things that happen to us are a mix of these three variables—a particular cross-section in time and space, plus our mindset at that moment. The single variable in that mix that we cannot control is time. And this is why any success should be honored with gratitude—because no matter how much we like to believe in our own efficacy, time and timing still belongs to the grand universe. However, that means that we still can influence two of those three variables—the spaces we occupy and our state of mind. Opportunity given to a defeated or resistant state of mind cannot manifest into success. Similarly, enthusiam and motivation will struggle to manifest success in a resource deprived environment. So choose to be intentional in giving yourself the best opportunities to succeed at whatever it is you desire by optimizing what you can in your life. Then you trust and leave the rest to the universe that when the time is right, you will be ready.

FARTHER THAN THOUGHT

FROM A STUDIO IN OAKLAND CALIFORNIA

CHOOSING TO BELIEVE

At some point, quietly or all at once, every human being looks up at the sky and feels the smallness of their body against the vastness of everything else. We all arrive here by different doors — religion, science, heartbreak, wonder — but eventually, we meet the same question: *What is all of this?* And beneath that: *Why am I here inside of it?* It is one thing to be told stories about God. It is another thing entirely to stand inside of your life, inside of your joy or your suffering, and need to know for yourself. To need it to feel real. To ache for proof not in books, but in the depths of your own existence. That ache—that holy hunger—might just be the beginning of faith.

And what exactly *is* faith? It is the questioning and then the choosing. Of an answer that satiates our soul. Deep down, we are aware that we may never *truly* know. But we do come to know an even bigger truth: that it may not *really* matter. That knowing may not even be the point. Not in the specifics anyway. What does seem to matter is how our truths about this universe allow for our most whole and abundant existences.

Because through all of the forms of this knowing— all the names and stories and prayers — what we are really reaching for is the same thing: an acceptance that there is a bigness that holds all of humanity — past, present, and future. This bigness, feeds us, nurtures us, steadies us, and paints us exquisite murals through the canyons and mountains. This bigness loves us in the truest sense of the word.

And maybe that is as far as many of us ever get it in understanding the infinite, in understanding God, or the universe.

And maybe—*just maybe*—that is more than enough.

FROM A STUDIO IN OAKLAND CALIFORNIA

YOU DO NOT NEED PERMISSION

You do not need permission to pursue your biggest, most beautiful life. The only thing you have to believe is that your soul is worth taking the chance on and then release control into the universe. You see, stability, as we have come to understand it, is a bit of a misnomer. In life, we are told to find security, something sturdy. However, the reality is that so much of what we believe is immovable can tilt in the blink of an eye. A more accurate description is that we become good at constructing balancing structures, each piece resting on the other. But those who have lost it all, know just how precarious those balancing structures really can be.

So then here is the question: If security is a cognitive fallacy, and the woven fabric of our constructed lives can become so fragile in an instant, should we then not be chasing the *most meaningful* lives possible? The ones where we embody the fullness of who we were meant to be? You see, a meaningful life is the opposite of fragile. It runs deep and comes from the most convicted parts of our beings. It is a life that thrives in truth. A life where we are brave with our hearts and honest about our desires. It is the life that is a manifestation of who we truly are. And the permission to surrender into oneself that way can only come from within.

THE TRUTH ABOUT CHANGING YOUR LIFE

When you decide to undo the fabric of your life,
turn it all upside down,
you will, at some point, wonder if you are losing your mind.
You will wonder if something vital has come undone.
You'll feel untethered,
like a structure collapsing mid-construction.
You'll be tempted to reach back, to grasp at old parts of it,
just to feel something *stable*.
Even if it's false.
Even if it's over.
But the truth is,
your soul knows exactly what it is looking for.
It has come to know a truth it cannot *un*know
that your old life cannot hold.
And once your awareness stretches,
your life and mind, as you knew it,
are already gone.
So yes, in that way, you *have* lost your mind.
The old parameters anyway.
But not in the way you fear.
Not into chaos,
but into *expansion*.
What is dying is the architecture of the old you.
To make way for what is meant to live inside
So the real question becomes,
"What will you do with this new expanded version?"

FROM A STUDIO IN OAKLAND CALIFORNIA

EXPANSION ANXIETY

The mind will do a funny little thing when you do step out onto the limb to reach for your most beautiful life: it will scream at you over and over again, *We are not safe here*. It will do this with such intensity that you will wonder if you have made a wrong turn. And if you don't turn back? It may swing itself into full-blown apathy. The kind of apathy where the weight of what you are carrying can be numbed. This place feels a bit better because at least there's no more screaming. The problem is, while numb, effort toward *anything* feels pointless. You see what it is trying to do, don't you? Take you back to the old life that at least felt safer than the limb even if it was completely misfit.

As hard as it is to tolerate, you must choose to allow the screaming. You must choose to *feel* it because that means you are also feeling your hope, and truth, and purpose, and ache of resilience that is coursing through your veins from all that you have already overcome. In truth, with each step you take further on the limb, it will become quieter and quieter. It does not mean you harm; it just does not know yet that you can fly.

ENIA OAKS

WHERE SKY MEETS THE OCEAN

There are moments in our lives that seem to stretch themselves so wide between now and the universe that it feels like we are standing at the very edge of existence—where the known world dissolves into something vast, something undefinable. It happens in the quiet just before dawn, when the weight of all of our past selves press against the present moment. It happens in grief, in love, in longing so deep it rearranges the shape of our souls.

To be alive is to stand at this edge over and over again, peering into the abyss of the infinite—of all that was, all that is, all that could have been, and all that will never be. It is the unbearable beauty of knowing that everything you touch, everything you love, will one day be dust. Even your own flesh. It is the strange, holy ache of being a fleeting thing in a world that keeps moving. But in that ache is the very essence of our human experience. The tangible layers of an intangible universe.

FROM A STUDIO IN OAKLAND CALIFORNIA

MEET ME ON THE LIMB

The truth is that many of us *do* spend our lives running from our inner selves. We find places, relationships, and careers that never demand we look inward or attempt to honor our beings. We fear what we might find—partially because society has given us parameters for what might be acceptable—so we keep our eyes straight ahead and our feet planted. We create microcosms of what a full life might look like and convince ourselves that we are content living a diluted version. The result? Our inner self slowly involutes until we become completely disconnected from it and all of its power.

When you leave a comfort zone, you step out onto a limb, your only true lifeline is your fortitude within. If you have spent no time challenging and nurturing the part of you that stretches to meet discomfort—your inner resilience—you have no evidence of your inner resolve. Without this evidence, there is no basis for self-trust. And in order to build either, you must first be willing to look inward. Because seeking discomfort or change without the promise of a connected and activated inner self would be an act of masochism. You must ask yourself consequential questions and be willing to explore answers that demand more of you. There are frightening expansions you must first withstand, a steadiness within yourself you must first learn to cultivate that will shelter your soul when your outside world has not quite yet caught up to the one inside. You must have learned to challenge all of the parameters of your life as you have lived it. And learn to fail and stand up over and over. Otherwise, you are destined to remain the same: living life far below the level of your true desires and potential.

When we avoid this work—when we refuse to turn inward—we tether our sense of security to everything *but* ourselves. We make external circumstances the foundation of our stability, hoping that relationships, careers, or fleeting affirmations will sustain us. But when life inevitably shifts—when loss, failure, or change arrive—we are left untethered, unable to trust in our own ability to withstand the storm. The only way out of this fragile existence is through *reconnection*. To sit with ourselves, to ask the hard deeply uncomfortable questions, and build resilience not through external validation, but through the consistent act of showing up for our inner world. Because when we do this—when we cultivate strength from within—we stop seeking false refuge in places that were never built to hold us in our wholeness. We give ourselves the foundation to go out onto the ledges and heights that allow our most beautiful lives.

FROM A STUDIO IN OAKLAND CALIFORNIA

THE ONE

We often talk about meeting "the one" as an event that happens *to us*. That it is this occurrence that we encounter outside of ourselves. The more I progress through life, the more I realize that it is more likely first an event or occurrence that happens *within* us.

The idea that there is a person who will be *just so* that all of the walls we have built inside of ourselves will just dissolve, does not feel completely honest. Because in reality, I have met many beautiful souls. We all have. So it can't be the meeting or just the other person. It seems that the experience of meeting "the one" first happens when we step into that space inside of ourselves. The space where we are ready to truly and deeply connect, through sovereignty of our soul and the allowance of the sovereignty of another's.

The space where we stand rooted in our belief of our own worthiness. Where we don't run from our own demons but also do not permit them to ruin things and make a mess. Yes some people will be better able to wrap their arms much wider and tighter around all of that we are.

But it seems that first we must have learned to wrap our own arms around ourselves first. Because however then could we ever accept being held in that way?

WHAT I WOULD'VE TOLD YOU SOONER

There are things in life that no one tells you early enough: You don't have to suffer to be worthy. You are allowed to want more—not because you've proven yourself, but because desire is the language of your soul.

The thing you are afraid will break you probably will. But the "you" you know was meant to be broken—over and over, throughout your life. That's how you know you're living. Growing. Evolving.

There are people who will leave simply to make space. And your body is wiser than you've been taught to believe. Your sensitivity? It is a superpower. Life will surprise you with beauty so exquisite it will make your knees weak. And most of what you're worrying about right now? It will sort itself out. Not because you force it. In fact, *never* when you force it. But it will work out because all of life's experiences are temporary—and it has a rhythm that favors those who stay present.

And here's another thing no one will tell you out loud: *All of this is made up.* All of it. The labels we give ourselves. The dividers we put between us and other people. The rules that keep you small. The timelines. The ladders to nowhere. Reality's only truth is this about humans: You are alive. You are conscious. And you are carrying a soul that is curious and yearning.

The rest? Made up. So free yourself and live from *that* truth alone. Leave the rest where it belongs—in the mental frameworks of those who still choose to believe in it. You? You are allowed to be free. That's the beauty of life. You always have been.

END

ABOUT THE AUTHOR

Enia Oaks is a writer, physician, and lifelong observer of the quiet beauty in being human.

Trained as emergency medicine physician, her work has always lived at the intersection of care in crisis and witness, tending to the rawest moments of people's lives while searching for meaning in her own.

Her writing is rooted in emotional honesty, spiritual reflection, and deep reverence for the human experience. She writes to meet readers in the tender middle of their own becoming.

From a Studio in Oakland, California: 108 Notes on Existence is her first book.

www.ingramcontent.com/pod-product-compliance
Lightning Source LLC
Chambersburg PA
CBHW030448100526
44580CB00002B/29